THE VIP JOB SEARCH

VISION, INITIATIVE, PRAYER

by Katherine Mychajluk

Trilogy Christian Publishers

A Wholly Owned Subsidiary of Trinity Broadcasting Network

2442 Michelle Drive |Tustin, CA 92780

Copyright © 2025 by Katherine Mychajluk

Unless otherwise indicated, all scripture quotations are from the King James Version of the Bible. Public domain. Scripture quotations marked AMPCE are taken from the Amplified Bible, Copyright © 1954, 1958, 1962, 1964, 1965, 1987 by The Lockman Foundation. Used by permission. Scripture quotations marked ESV are taken from the ESV® Bible (The Holy Bible, English Standard Version®), copyright © 2001 by Crossway Bibles, a publishing ministry of Good News Publishers. Used by permission. All rights reserved. Scripture quotations marked NIV are taken from the Holy Bible, New International Version®, NIV®. Copyright © 1973, 1978, 1984, 2011 by Biblica, Inc.TM Used by permission of Zondervan. All rights reserved worldwide. www.zondervan.com. The "NIV" and "New International Version" are trademarks registered in the United States Patent and Trademark Office by Biblica, Inc.TM Scripture quotations marked NLT are taken from the Holy Bible, New Living Translation, copyright © 1996, 2004, 2015 by Tyndale House Foundation. Used by permission of Tyndale House Publishers, Inc., Carol Stream, Illinois 60188. All rights reserved. Scripture quotations marked NKJV are taken from the New King James Version®. Copyright © 1982 by Thomas Nelson. Used by permission. All rights reserved. Scripture quotations marked TLB are taken from The Living Bible copyright © 1971. Used by permission of Tyndale House Publishers, a Division of Tyndale House Ministries, Carol Stream, Illinois 60188. All rights reserved.

All rights reserved, including the right to reproduce this book or portions thereof in any form whatsoever.

For information, address Trilogy Christian Publishing

Rights Department, 2442 Michelle Drive, Tustin, Ca 92780.

Trilogy Christian Publishing/ TBN and colophon are trademarks of Trinity Broadcasting Network.

For information about special discounts for bulk purchases, please contact Trilogy Christian Publishing.

Trilogy Disclaimer: The views and content expressed in this book are those of the author and may not necessarily reflect the views and doctrine of Trilogy Christian Publishing or the Trinity Broadcasting Network.

10 9 8 7 6 5 4 3 2 1

Library of Congress Cataloging-in-Publication Data is available.

ISBN 979-8-89333-840-9 | ISBN 979-8-89333-841-6 (ebook)

Dedication

I dedicate this book to my earthly father, John Mychajluk, who possessed deep faith, a strong belief and trust in God.

During World War II, in a time of turmoil and uncertainty, John fled from Ukraine to Germany, and eventually, he settled in the United States. As a teenager, I asked my father why he decided to come to the United States. His simple yet profound reason for moving to the US was: "I heard there were jobs there."

This book is a tribute to John's unwavering faith and the quiet strength it takes to start anew, honoring a legacy of perseverance and the belief in a brighter future. It's a story that resonates with many, reminding us of the courage it takes to chase a dream across continents and the enduring power of hope. This reflects the aspirations of many who, in the past and today, seek a better life for themselves and their families.

Acknowledgments

I would like to acknowledge the following people God has blessed me with who have made a significant impact on my life:

- Former Senior Pastor Dr. Steven Treash, of Black Rock Church, Fairfield, Connecticut, for over forty years in his leadership role, demonstrating his unwavering commitment to Christian growth in our church, with the staff, and in the community.

- Current Senior Pastor Josh Feay, of Black Rock Church, Fairfield, Connecticut: Josh has been on staff for over twenty years. Josh encourages people of all ages to develop a personal relationship with Jesus as he shares the good news of the gospel in his weekly sermons.

- I would like to congratulate my brother, Klaus Janson, for his induction into the 2024 Eisner Awards Hall of Fame. I would also like to thank him for designing the cover of my book, as well as for his wisdom, support, and encouragement in the pursuit of my dream.

- Louise Simpson, a powerhouse Christian prayer warrior. Her countless hours of support in balancing the Christian and secular aspects have been invaluable.

The VIP Job Search

- Superhero Mike Shavel, a career counselor and advocate at the local Department of Labor Unemployment Office. I consider Mike a caped crusader with a superpower of encouragement and inspiration for everyone.

- John Pacheco, LCSW, LADC: In his role as a career and job coach, John has been pivotal in the professional landscape of my career. He brings a wealth of knowledge, offering guidance tailored to individual needs and aspirations.

- Angel Garcia, Black Rock Prayer Team Leadership: As members of Black Rock Church, Angel and I found ourselves unemployed at the same time. I appreciate the entire prayer team for their commitment to pray daily for our church family.

- Black Rock Board of Elders for the God-driven decisions to always follow the word of God in the Bible. Black Rock Church is a beacon of light in our area.

- Ted Pizzo, Founder of Northeast Executive Advisory Group: Ted is a leader, organizer, and great listener. He provides individuals who are unemployed or looking for a career change with direction to achieve their goals.

- Mark Mingle, Account Executive at Trilogy Christian Publishing, for assisting with the navigation and thrilling world of publishing. Mark is a great strategist and turns

Acknowledgments

prospects into loyal patrons, with the mission of TBN at his core.

- The production team at Trilogy Publishing, especially Allison Dyer, Trilogy Project Manager. The publishing team is where the ink meets the paper, and the layout team transforms a writer's manuscript into a page-turning masterpiece.

- A heartfelt thank-you to the Trinity Broadcasting Network leadership team for creating Trilogy Christian Publishing. Thank you for making Christian publishing a reality, for the opportunity, and for furthering God's kingdom.

Table of Contents

My Personal Mission Statement 11

Preface. 13

Chapter 1: Unemployed 17

Chapter 2: Make a Plan. 29

Chapter 3: Get Organized: Your Job Search Toolkit. 49

Chapter 4: Your New Day Job 69

Chapter 5: Activate Your Plan. 91

Chapter 6: It's All About Your Mindset 109

Chapter 7: Community of Support 129

Chapter 8: Interviews and the Internet1 139

Chapter 9: Reflect on the Process 163

Chapter 10: Keep an Open Mind 183

Chapter 11: Landing the Job. 201

Chapter 12: Continue to Learn 217

My Personal Mission Statement

This book was written to encourage you to uncover your God-given strengths and talents in your job and career. The journey will be deeply personal and lead to self-discovery. As you begin each day in prayer, the Holy Spirit will guide you through the job search process.

Preface

As an HR professional and Christian, I faced significant challenges in my career, navigating through corporate changes while trying to maintain my integrity and faith. It's been a challenge to hold onto my principles, even when pressured to act unethically. My motto has always been, "I'm not going to jail for anybody," which reflects my strong commitment to doing the right thing despite difficult circumstances. I'm sure many others have faced similar ethical dilemmas in their professional lives.

While unemployed, I experienced some troubling times during the interview process. It's disheartening to experience and witness the lack of empathy and respect shown to candidates, especially during such vulnerable times. Unfortunately, some individuals and organizations may resort to unkind behavior out of fear, insecurity, or a misguided sense of superiority. Although the journey may be challenging, standing in faith can inspire positive change and set an example for others.

When I noticed people behaving badly during the interview process, I viewed the situation as receiving information about the company. Rather than taking it personally, I saw this as an example of God showing me who these people were, knowing that He would not want me to work in such an environment.

It's unfortunate that some companies allow bad behavior to persist. It does make you wonder about the awareness and accountability of their leadership teams. On the bright side, not all interviews were like that. Your focus and trust need to be on God and not on people or their behavior. Human beings are flawed and with sin. Keep your eyes on Jesus and rely on your faith. If God wants you to have the job, He will make it happen. Follow the promptings of the Holy Spirit.

Was the job search process easy? Absolutely not. Did I want to go through the process? No, not at all. Did I ask God why did this have to happen to me? Why did I have to go through this? Yes. I prayed all the time, and sometimes I received a response through the Holy Spirit, and sometimes I did not. However, I knew I had to keep on going as I was curious as to what God had in store for me. I made a decision on day one of unemployment that I would never give up.

My motivation for writing this book is heartfelt and full of compassion for others. I still witness individuals today struggling with the job search process. Some are afraid to follow their dreams; others desire a career change but are frozen in fear.

The loss of multiple jobs in my HR career provided an opportunity to reflect deeply on my faith and the search for meaning in my life. The plus side of unemployment and going through a rigorous job search process is that I found comfort through a

Preface

deeper relationship with God and Jesus. The freedom we have in the United States can sometimes lead to a sense of self-sufficiency, making it easy to overlook the spiritual aspects of life.

Finding our purpose is a journey that many of us undertake. We often turn to various resources, such as self-help books, to guide us. It's important to remember that everyone's path is unique, and seeking answers through faith, introspection, and learning can be a fulfilling and life-long process.

The stories in the Bible can resonate with our modern life powerfully. The Bible offers timeless wisdom and relatable stories despite the differences in technology and lifestyle in the Old and New Testaments.

The struggles and triumphs of Bible characters can resonate deeply with our own experiences today. Whether it's dealing with family dynamics, financial stress, or career uncertainties, the lessons and principles found in the Bible can provide comfort and direction. It's a reminder that, at our core, human experiences and emotions remain consistent across the ages.

I wrote this book to share my insights and perspective with others. I am hopeful that my book is inspiring as I have a deep passion for helping others find guidance and support in their lives.

Chapter 1:

Unemployed

"He gives justice to all who are treated unfairly."

Psalm 103:6 (TLB)

Losing a job is a traumatic experience. It feels like a sudden blow that shatters your sense of security and identity. You may ask yourself, *How could this happen to me? I did everything right: I worked hard, I was loyal, and I was successful. How can they just discard me like this?* Many people, when they lose their jobs or careers, feel hurt and betrayed by their employers.

When we face difficult situations, we often want to know the reasons behind them. We may think that knowing the reasons would make us feel better. We need to look to the Trinity for knowledge, comfort, and wisdom in all circumstances. The doctrine of the Trinity means that there is one God who eternally exists as three distinct persons—the Father, Son, and Holy Spirit. Stated differently, God is one in essence and three in person. These definitions express three crucial truths: (1) the Father, Son, and Holy Spirit are distinct persons, (2) each person is fully God, and (3) there is only one God. By praying regularly and focusing on God's Word, it can help you calm your mind, reduce stress, and enhance your well-being. Refer to the Scripture referenced under each chapter title in this book as you think about your goals and aspirations for your job search and your life. May these Scriptures fill you with faith-filled expectation in your plan to achieve your goals.

When we experience any type of loss, it is a painful sting to our self-esteem, and we have a human desire to react and protect ourselves. Hurtful attacks on our self-esteem may result in anger and lashing out at people in an attempt to try to put some control back into our lives. No matter how difficult a situation may be, change is inevitable and even necessary. You may have known deep down inside for a long period of time that your current job was not a good fit for you or your talents. However, you stayed in the position because you were too comfortable. You may have longed for a different position or work in a different career, but your financial commitments kept you from making that change.

Losing a job can be a traumatic experience for anyone, regardless of their age or career stage. It is one of the top ten stressful events that a person can face in life. Many people identify themselves with their work and feel a loss as to who they are—their sense of purpose—when they experience a job loss. Some people may also feel ashamed or guilty as if they are a failure or have done something wrong. This is not always the case. In many instances, job loss is due to factors beyond one's control, such as economic downturns, organizational changes, or technological shifts. These are not personal failures but challenges that many people have to face in today's dynamic and uncertain world.

In past years, baby boomers born between 1946 and 1964 were rewarded with loyalty, job security, and stability. They expected to stay with one employer for their entire career and enjoy the benefits of a pension and retirement plan. However, in the past decade or so, many baby boomers have faced the harsh reality of layoffs and downsizing their expectations. They may feel betrayed, angry, or disillusioned by their employers.

Losing my first job was a painful experience that revealed the true nature of people. Instead of being supportive and encouraging, a few acted as if I had a contagious disease. This resulted in a few friends avoiding me—afraid somehow they would "catch" my unfortunate predicament of a job loss. It's as if I had a case of "unemployment flu" in which there was no cure. There is no vaccine to protect your dreams, goals, and career aspirations.

In the last ten to fifteen years, job loss has increasingly become more common. However, recruiters and HR professionals have not yet grasped or accepted what is occurring in the corporate world. That is, until it happens to them and they have a bite of the reality sandwich. Some recruiters, hiring managers, and HR professionals can be quite insensitive and lack compassion.

Human Resource professionals often scrutinize employment gaps on resumes, which can influence their decision-making process. To mitigate the stigma of employment gaps, utilize a strategic resume design and clear communication in your cover letter. Then there are others who have more compassion, knowledge, and understanding. That is, there are HR professionals who can actually recognize the skills and abilities you have to offer and will take a chance on interviewing and hiring an individual who is unemployed. There are many hurdles and challenges to overcome when a person is unemployed. Through daily prayer and the guidance of the Holy Spirit, we are able to overcome fear and regain peace through the unemployment process.

As an HR professional, I continued to persevere and go on interviews. It was hard being in God's will while you were wait-

Unemployed

ing and wanting something so badly. There are many things that we think we need or want in life; however, God knows best.

Whether the person was a Christian or a non-Christian friend in my life, I was especially surprised on a number of occasions regarding the comments I would receive from individuals about being out of work for such an extended period of time. The questions received from Christians could be more biting at times—than from non-Christians. A friend of mine who is a Christian once asked me why I was having trouble finding a new job despite having many interviews. I explained that there are a number of factors involved during an interview process, and it comes down to a "numbers" game. For instance, some employers may have biases based on age or appearance. Moreover, some employers may not be willing to pay a fair or competitive salary or even match the previous salary of the applicant. There are a multitude of reasons why a person is not selected for a position, and we may never understand why. This is where the torment may begin for many people and they give up and stop interviewing. As Christians, what we do understand is that God loves us and that He is in control. The Trinity understands all our struggles and provides guidance—when we ask—every step of the way.

There is never a good time to lose a job, no matter what stage of life it happens. Whether when first starting out your career or when you are closer to retirement. It is a bump in the road and interferes with whatever plans you may have moving forward in your life. However, it is not a stop sign.

One of the most common pieces of advice that successful executives give is to always think and plan ahead for your next career move. When do we begin this process? When you just started a new job, the next step is to start thinking about your next role. Where would you like to go next? What does your career look like in the future? Most of us do not follow that process, as we seek security and comfort. We know there are no guarantees in life and our only security is in Jesus.

I wrote this book for believers and non-believers alike to provide a practical guide with an HR perspective on what to do—how to begin the complicated world of your new full-time job: your job search. I also provide tips on how to succeed in your job search process, step by step.

Life is full of uncertainties and challenges that we cannot predict or control. But we have a loving Creator who knows our destiny and guides us along the way. We cannot rely on our own wisdom or strength to face the difficulties of life. We need to trust in the Trinity, who gives us peace, knowledge, and guidance.

Open your mind and change your mindset. What is your perception and response to the world of work around you? A mindset can be defined as a set of beliefs, attitudes, and assumptions that shape our thoughts, feelings, and actions. There are different types of mindsets, such as fixed, growth, positive, and negative, that can affect our performance, motivation, and well-being.

What is your perception about the world of work? What motivated you at your last position? Is it intrinsic motivations such as personal growth, curiosity, or the pursuit of happiness? Or is it extrinsic motivations such as financial incentives, social recognition, or external rewards? Motivations can shift over time due to changes in personal circumstances and societal values. Different life stages can profoundly impact one's motivations, leading to a reevaluation of goals and aspirations.

People with a growth mindset see challenges as opportunities to grow, embrace feedback as a way to improve, and persist in the face of setbacks. They also tend to have a positive outlook on life and a high sense of self-efficacy.

Losing your job can be a stressful and challenging experience, but it can also be an opportunity to take a break and recharge your batteries. Some people may choose to travel or go on a vacation after becoming unemployed, and that's perfectly fine. However, it's important to have a clear and realistic plan for your job search before you pack your bags. That way, you can enjoy your trip without worrying about how to start the process when you come back.

Having a written plan for your job search can help you stay focused, motivated, and organized. It can also help you track your progress and measure your results. A good plan should include your career goals, your target employers, your networking strategies, your resume and cover letter, and your interview preparation. You should also set a timeline and a budget for your job search and review your plan regularly to make any adjustments.

While you are looking for a new job, you may also want to explore other possibilities for your career. Maybe you are not satisfied with your current field, or maybe you want to try something new. You can use this time to do some self-assessment and research on different occupations that match your skills, interests, and values. You can also take some online tests or quizzes to discover more about yourself and your career preferences. You may find out that you are on the right track or that you need to make some changes. Either way, you will gain more clarity and confidence about your career direction.

The time frame for being out of work varies from state to state, depending on your field, your experience, or your credentials—it also depends on the career opportunities in your area.

Another tool in your "job search kit" is your networking group. Networking is important in your career development and business relationships. I recommend joining civic, community,

Unemployed

and business councils to create a network, whether employed or unemployed. Networking should be part of your regular activities as it takes time to build a network of trust and mutual benefit. By doing so, you are preparing for future opportunities.

It is imperative that skills remain updated at all times. The world is full of amazing people who are doing excellent work, and sometimes, they face the risk of losing their jobs. This can happen for various reasons, such as the economic situation, the tax burden, or the profitability of their employers.

We all have unique gifts and talents given to us by God, and we must remember that we are working unto God and not unto man. We strive to do our best, and it is a journey of learning and growing.

Ask God to reveal His plan for you in your job search and for your future. Scripture tells us in 1 Peter 5:7 (NKJV) to "cast your care upon Him." As my circumstances became more challenging, I decided to lean further into my faith. As a result, my faith became stronger; however, it was not easy. I knew that God was in control and that He loved me and would provide for me, even after my unemployment benefits ran out and I depleted my savings account.

Searching for a job can be a time-consuming and exhausting process. You may have to spend several hours a day browsing through job boards, sending applications, and following up with employers.

Do not complain about being out of work. Someone once said, "If you complain, you remain." Focus on the good things in your life. Gratitude is a key factor during the unemployment process. Be grateful for what you have—focus on what is good in your life. Focus on what you have, not on what you don't have. That takes changing your mindset, changing your focus, basically—changing the way you think. Challenge your brain—your thought process—to think differently. Unless you think differently about your life—changing your thinking about how to approach the process—nothing will change. The change has to occur on the inside—not on the outside. Find positive ways to relieve stress while unemployed as you go through the job search process.

During my period of unemployment, I enrolled in various courses offered by the unemployment office, such as resume writing, interviewing skills, Excel and Microsoft Office skills, and LinkedIn. This was an efficient use of my time and improved my job prospects as I learned more skills. I became more marketable in the ever-evolving job market.

Your brain is a powerful tool that can shape your reality, but sometimes, it can also hold you back from achieving your goals and living your best life. One way to develop a more positive mindset is to read Scripture every day, which will give you a greater perspective. Here are some steps to begin the process:

- Repeat God's promises multiple times throughout the day.
- Replace negative statements with positive statements.
- Create goals with realistic expectations.
- Practice gratitude and optimism daily.
- Anticipate miracles as God moves in your life.

Persevering through difficulty is a crucial skill that allows us to overcome challenges and grow as individuals. By adopting the above strategies, we can navigate life's curveballs with courage and resilience.

HR insider tip. When you receive notice that your job is being "downsized," "outsourced," or that the "company is moving in a different direction," it is crucial to examine all documents provided by Human Resources. The documentation typically includes details of a (possible) severance package, payout of accrued vacation time, costs, and the termination date for health insurance benefits. Understanding the documentation received is essential for managing a successful transition period and managing it effectively. For clarification on any points that are unclear, it is advisable to consider consulting with a legal or career professional if necessary.

Chapter 2:

Make a Plan

"Where there is no vision, the people perish."

Proverbs 29:18

    Embracing new experiences and stepping outside of one's comfort zone can indeed be a powerful strategy in life and job searching. It fosters adaptability and resilience, qualities that are highly valued in the workplace. Journaling is an excellent example of a personal development activity that can enhance one's mental well-being. Exercising may also contribute to a more positive outlook and increased energy level, which can be infectious in interviews and networking opportunities.

Writing your goals in a journal or notebook serves as a powerful picture of what you are striving towards. These goals provide clarity and direction as to what is important to you. This helps you not only focus but stay accountable in making your goal a reality. Focusing on your goals and reviewing them daily helps you affirm through your eyes of faith.

Effective time management and organization can bring structure to the day, making tasks seem more manageable. It is essential to recognize the value of a structured job search strategy, which includes:

- establishing a daily routine
- setting achievable goals
- being open to learning, and
- adjusting tactics based on the job market's feedback.

Economic cycles and job markets fluctuate, but with a steadfast commitment to your goals, self-confidence, and faith, you'll be prepared to seize opportunities when they arise. Your unique skills and experiences are your strengths, and with persistence, the right opportunity will present itself.

Make a Plan

The job search journey is a testament to one's persistence and perseverance. Included in that journey is an effective time-management plan, which includes a calendar and daily tasks. The most effective daily task and the most effective tool in your "job search toolbox" is prayer. Information on your job search toolbox will be provided later in this chapter.

In times of uncertainty, such as unemployment, establishing a routine that includes daily prayer can be a source of comfort and strength. It serves as a grounding practice that can alleviate stress and foster a sense of stability. Building a habit of turning to prayer for guidance and support can enhance self-confidence and resilience, providing the inner resources needed to handle unexpected life events with grace. Moreover, prayer can inspire the perseverance and creativity needed to explore new opportunities in a challenging job market. By integrating prayer into daily life, not just during periods of unemployment but as a life-long practice, individuals may find themselves naturally dedicating more time to connecting with God through a relationship with Jesus. This spiritual connection enriches a person's personal growth and helps them navigate through unexpected life events.

Resilience is indeed a crucial trait in a competitive job market. It's the ability to bounce back from setbacks, adapt well to change, and keep going in the face of adversity. Setting aside daily time for personal reflection and spiritual growth is a powerful way to build this resilience. Through prayer, quiet moments can provide the strength and perspective needed to persevere in your career journey. As this practice becomes a habit, it often leads to a deeper connection with God, one's faith, and values, which can be a source of comfort and motivation during challenging times. Remember, the path to success is often a marathon, not a sprint, and nurturing your spiritual well-being through a relationship with Jesus is an integral part of maintaining endurance and focus.

Maintaining mental and emotional well-being during a job search is indeed crucial. A varied routine can help you stay engaged and prevent burnout. Consider starting your day with a morning ritual that energizes you, such as prayer, reading, and exercise. Allocate specific time blocks for job search activities, including networking, applying for jobs, and enhancing your skills through online courses or certifications. Remember to include breaks to refresh your mind, perhaps a walk with God to simply tell Him what is on your mind and what you need. End your day with a review of accomplishments and set goals for the next day. This balance of activities can help you stay focused and motivated throughout your job search journey.

Make a Plan

Sample Daily Job Search Action Plan

Action: *Schedule:*

1. Alarm set; wake up.   7:00 a.m.

2. Make coffee.   7:15 a.m.

3. Prayer time.   7:30 a.m.

4. Go for a walk; exercise.   8:00 a.m.

5. Shower, get dressed, breakfast.   8:30 a.m.

6. Arrive at your job search desk.   9:15 a.m.

7. Apply for unemployment benefits.   9:30 a.m.

8. Craft a personal mission statement.   11:20 a.m.

9. Meet a friend for lunch.   12:30 p.m.

10. Print your resume and review.   2:00 p.m.

11. Research cover letter and resume styles.   3:15 p.m.

12. Take a break. Play with the dog.   4:05 p.m.

13. Create tomorrow's schedule.   4:35 p.m.

The VIP Job Search

Approaching a job search with a one-day-at-a-time mindset can be incredibly beneficial. It helps maintain focus and reduces the overwhelming feeling that can come with considering all the potential outcomes at once. By concentrating on the present, you can dedicate your energy to crafting tailored applications, preparing for interviews, and enhancing your skills—actions that are directly within your control. This approach aligns with many philosophical and spiritual teachings that emphasize the importance of living in the present moment. It's a practice of mindfulness that not only aids in a job search but can also improve overall well-being. Remember, each day is a new opportunity to take a step toward your goals, and by focusing on the tasks at hand, you can make steady progress in your career journey.

Worry is from the evil one to make us stressed, and if we are stressed, we are preoccupied and not able to focus on our job search or God's plan for our lives. When you find yourself worrying about the future...stop yourself and pray. Pick up your Bible or devotional and read as God's Word has a calming effect. You will be comforted by the Holy Spirit as you are reaching out to God through prayer.

Throughout history, many have found solace, wisdom, and comfort in the Scriptures of their faith. These texts often serve as a guiding light through the complexities of life, offering insights and teachings that have been reflected upon for generations.

They provide a source of strength and encouragement, helping individuals to navigate their personal journeys and find peace amidst turmoil. For those who believe, biblical writings continue to be a wellspring of spiritual nourishment and a testament to the enduring human search for meaning and connection.

Managing stress while unemployed is a significant challenge for many, and various strategies can be effective in mitigating its impact. Engaging in prayer, reading Scripture, or meditating on devotional texts are ways that can help center the mind and provide a sense of peace and direction. These practices can serve as a reminder of a higher purpose and provide a framework for coping with the uncertainties of life, including the stresses of job searching. It's important for each individual to find the approach that best supports their well-being and aligns with their values and beliefs.

The job search journey can indeed be a solitary one, where the support and understanding of those around us might not always be readily available. It's a path that can test one's resilience and patience, especially in a competitive job market where the process can be lengthy and responses from potential employers may be infrequent. It's crucial to build a network of support, whether through career counselors, support groups, or online communities, where experiences are shared and understood. It's also important to remember that this phase is temporary and part of a larger journey. Seeking comfort in God through your faith can provide a sense of peace and strength, offering solace during challenging times. It's a personal reflection of one's beliefs and trust in the Holy Trinity's plan for their life's path.

The concept of a personal relationship with God through Jesus is often expressed as a journey of faith, where an individual seeks a deeper understanding and connection with the Trinity. This spiritual pursuit is seen as a path to gaining insight into one's own life. Many find comfort in the belief that their thoughts and desires are known to God, and this connection can bring guidance and solace. The idea that one only needs to reach out and ask for His help and to build a relationship with Him reflects a universal hope for support and companionship in the journey of life.

Life's unexpected turns can indeed be challenging and sometimes overwhelming. It's natural to feel a mix of emotions, including anger and confusion, when plans go awry despite hard work and dedication. Seeking comfort in faith, sharing your feelings, and focusing on the strength of your beliefs are sources of resilience. It's important to remember that while the path may change, it doesn't mean the journey is over. New opportunities can arise from change, and with support from loved ones and personal faith, one can navigate through these transitions. Embracing the unpredictability of life while holding onto hope and perseverance can lead to new avenues and experiences that contribute to personal growth and fulfillment.

Make a Plan

Job loss and the subsequent search for new employment can be an emotionally taxing experience. It's natural to feel a range of emotions, including anger and frustration. However, it's crucial to channel these emotions constructively. Holding onto anger can inadvertently affect one's job search, as it may come across during interviews or networking opportunities. I heard a saying once from Joyce Meyer where she said, "If you complain, you remain," which underscores the importance of adopting a forward-thinking mindset. Instead of dwelling on the past, focusing on the future and the opportunities it holds can be more beneficial. Seeking professional counseling can be a valuable step for those finding it challenging to move past their emotions. Moreover, maintaining a professional demeanor when discussing past employers is essential, as negative comments can reflect poorly on an individual's character and potentially jeopardize future job prospects.

It's important to address these feelings beforehand, as they are perceptible even in virtual settings like Zoom or Teams interviews. Recruiters are adept at interpreting these cues and may consider them when deciding on a candidate's suitability for a role. Therefore, dealing with negative emotions is not just about personal well-being but also about enhancing job prospects by presenting oneself as a composed and adaptable professional.

Managing stress during periods of unemployment is indeed vital for overall well-being. It's essential to acknowledge the emotional impact of job loss, which can range from shock and disbelief to anxiety and worry. Adopting coping strategies such as maintaining a regular sleep schedule, engaging in physical exercise, and finding purposeful activities can significantly mitigate stress levels. Financial planning is also crucial; assessing one's financial situation and creating a budget can provide a sense of control and security. Additionally, it's beneficial to establish a structured daily routine that includes time for job search activities, rest, and leisure to preserve mental and physical health. Seeking social support from friends, family, or support groups can provide emotional comfort and practical assistance during the job search process. Remember, while the stress of unemployment is challenging, there are effective methods to manage it and maintain resilience.

The job search process indeed mirrors the meticulous planning and tool selection necessary for any successful project. Just as a well-equipped toolbox is essential for home improvement tasks, a robust set of resources is crucial for navigating the job market. This toolkit may include a polished resume, a compelling cover letter, a professional online presence, and a network of contacts. Each of these tools serves a specific purpose, much like a hammer or screwdriver, and when used effectively, they can significantly enhance the prospects of landing a desired position. Moreover, just as a gardener cultivates their garden, a job seeker must nurture their career prospects with continuous learning

Make a Plan

and skill development to stay relevant in a competitive job landscape.

The "job search toolbox" is a comprehensive suite of resources and tools designed to assist individuals in navigating the complexities of the job market. Drawing from both professional HR expertise and personal experience, this toolbox encompasses a range of strategies and technologies that have demonstrated success in the job search process. It includes social media networking for expanding professional connections and digital tools for organizing job applications and creating compelling resumes and cover letters. By leveraging these tools, you, as the job seekers, can efficiently identify opportunities, engage with potential employers, and ultimately secure employment. Your "job search toolbox" includes:

1. *Daily morning prayer*

2. *Your personal mission statement*

3. *Cover letters* (with keywords specific for each job application)

4. *Your resume* (with keywords specific for each job application)

5. *Your LinkedIn profile*

6. *Networking*

7. *Professional and self-development*

Embarking on a job search can be a transformative journey, one that not only leads to a new position but also fosters personal growth and professional development. The tools and techniques outlined in a comprehensive job search guide are invaluable assets that serve multiple purposes. They are designed to refine your approach to finding employment, enhancing your ability to present your skills and experiences effectively. Moreover, these tools are not just for securing a job; they are life skills that bolster your confidence and resilience in the face of career challenges. By mastering these tools, you equip yourself with a robust set of skills that prepare you for future endeavors, ensuring that you can navigate the job market with assurance and adaptability. Whether it's crafting a compelling resume, networking strategically, or acing interviews, each skill you acquire is a step toward a more secure and prosperous career path.

Acquiring new habits and skills, such as organization, task management, and planning, is a proactive approach to personal development. These skills are not only beneficial for day-to-day efficiency but are also highly valued in the workplace. During periods of unemployment, honing these abilities can be particularly advantageous. They can enhance your performance in job interviews, demonstrating to potential employers your capacity for self-improvement and effective time management. Furthermore, once you secure a new position, these skills will contribute to your success and productivity, proving that the effort invested in learning them has both immediate and long-term benefits.

Make a Plan

Prayer is often considered a vital component in the job search process for many individuals. It is seen as a source of strength, guidance, and patience, providing a sense of peace and clarity during times of uncertainty. The act of prayer can be a personal journey, aligning one's goals with a higher purpose and potentially opening doors to new opportunities. It is believed that through prayer, one can find the courage to face the challenges of job hunting, express fears and anxieties, and ultimately, receive guidance on the path to professional fulfillment.

Following prayer, a personal mission statement serves as a compass, guiding one's career trajectory. It encapsulates one's values, passions, and the "why" behind their career choices. Crafting a personal mission statement involves introspection to identify what is truly important, setting the stage for a career aligned with one's core values and life goals. It aids in decision-making, ensuring that each step taken is in service of one's long-term objectives. A well-articulated mission statement can provide direction during the job search, helping to communicate one's purpose and aspirations to potential employers.

Prayer is often considered a profound and personal tool in one's job search, offering strength, guidance, and a sense of peace during the process. It is believed to help individuals align their career goals with God's purpose for their lives and attract the right opportunities, acting as a beacon of hope and a source of comfort in times of uncertainty. Similarly, a personal mission statement is a powerful instrument in defining one's career trajectory. It encapsulates an individual's core values and aspirations, providing a clear direction and vision. Corporations use mission statements to unify and guide their employees toward a common goal. Individuals can use their personal mission statement to stay focused on their objectives and ensure that their actions are aligned with their faith, personal beliefs, and career ambitions. Both prayer and a personal mission statement can serve as vital components of a job search toolbox, each contributing to a *holistic* approach to personal and professional development.

A personal mission statement serves as a compass to guide you toward God's purpose for your life, encapsulating your core values, aspirations, and the essence of what drives you in your personal and professional life. It's a declaration of intent and philosophy, succinctly stating who you are and what you stand for. For example, "I am committed to fostering growth and learning, both in myself and others, to create a positive impact in every endeavor I undertake," or "My purpose is to live with integrity and make meaningful contributions that reflect my passion for serving God and His community." These statements anchor your actions and decisions, providing clarity and motivation as you navigate the journey of your career and personal growth. Crafting this statement thoughtfully can be a powerful exercise in self-reflection and intention-setting. Remember, it's not set in stone; as you evolve, so too can your mission statement.

Creating a personal mission statement is a powerful exercise that can provide clarity and direction for your life and career path. It encapsulates your values, goals, and aspirations, serving as a constant reminder of what you strive to achieve. By placing it prominently on your desk, it acts as a beacon, guiding you through the ebbs and flows of the job search journey. It's not just a piece of paper; it's a commitment to yourself, a written declaration of your intentions and purpose. When challenges arise, it reminds you of the bigger picture and the reasons behind your pursuit, helping to reignite your passion and drive. This practice of reflection and reaffirmation can be a cornerstone of personal development and professional growth.

Creating a personal mission statement is indeed a thoughtful process. It serves as a compass to guide your decisions and actions, reflecting your deepest values and aspirations. Start by reflecting on what matters most to you: What are your core values? What brings you fulfillment? Consider the legacy you want to leave and the impact you wish to have. As you brainstorm, look for themes and patterns that resonate with your sense of purpose. Write freely and without self-judgment, allowing your ideas to flow. Then, refine your statement over several drafts, honing in on the language that truly captures the essence of your unique mission. Remember, your personal mission statement is a living document that can evolve as you grow and gain new insights into your life's direction.

Here are a few examples of personal mission statements from successful ministry and business leaders:

- Joyce Meyer Ministries is called to "share the Gospel, disciple nations, and extend the love of Christ. Through media, we teach people how to apply biblical truth to every aspect of their lives and encourage God's people to serve the world around them. Through our mission's arm, Hand of Hope, we provide global humanitarian aid, feed the hungry, clothe the poor, minister to the elderly, widows, and orphans, and reach out to people of all ages and in all walks of life. Joyce Meyer Ministries is built on a foundation of faith, integrity, and dedicated supporters who share this call."

- Black Rock Church calls everyone to "Love God, love people, and serve our world."

- Habitat for Humanity's mission is "Seeking to put God's love into action, Habitat for Humanity brings people together to build homes, communities, and hope."

Creating a personal mission statement is a powerful way to clarify one's goals and values, acting as a compass to guide decision-making and goal-setting. It's a declaration of purpose that can help prioritize actions and give direction to life's journey. By dedicating time to prayer and reflection, one can find strength and clarity, reinforcing the importance of self-care and personal growth. This practice can lead to increased confidence and self-esteem, as it encourages individuals to live with intention and pursue their dreams with conviction. Conversely, recognizing and addressing bad habits is crucial, as they can impede progress and diminish self-worth. Thus, a mission statement is more than words; it's a commitment to living a life aligned with one's deepest convictions and aspirations.

The establishment of good habits is indeed a cornerstone of personal development and well-being. Consistency in practicing these habits solidifies them into routines that are difficult to break, thereby creating a virtuous cycle of positive behavior. The initial challenge of adopting new habits is often offset by the long-term benefits they bring, not only to one's physical and mental health but also in aligning daily actions with broader life goals. Reflecting on whether one's actions are contributing towards or detracting from these goals can be a powerful motivator for change. Cultivating habits that foster happiness and health, such as prayer, mindfulness, or gratitude, have transformative effects on one's life, reinforcing the notion that our thoughts and attitudes have a profound impact on our overall happiness. It's a continuous process of nurturing the good and weeding out the unhelpful, always with an eye on the kind of life one aspires to lead.

The journey through the job interview process is indeed a test of faith, patience, and perseverance. It's a path filled with various experiences that can be unexpected, challenging, and sometimes disheartening. It's important to approach this journey with resilience and a positive mindset, understanding that each step, each interview, and each moment of waiting contributes to personal and professional growth. While it's natural to feel a range of emotions, from excitement to frustration, it's crucial to stay focused on the ultimate goal and to learn from each experience. The support of faith, family, and friends can be a comforting and empowering presence during this time, providing strength and encouragement to continue moving forward. Remember, every interview is an opportunity to learn and improve, and with each attempt, you're one step closer to finding the right opportunity that aligns with your skills and aspirations. Keep striving, keep learning, and look to God our Father and lean on Him for the right job. God has the right job lined up for us. The right job is out there, waiting for the right moment to arrive.

The concept of striving to be the best version of oneself is a common theme in the pursuit of personal growth, ethical conduct, and the development of virtues such as kindness, patience, and humility. This pursuit is seen as a lifelong journey, where each individual is encouraged to reflect on their actions, seek wisdom, and contribute positively to the community around them. The idea that God created individuals with a purpose and

Make a Plan

seeks the best for them is an uplifting message that can inspire people to lead meaningful lives.

HR insider tip. *As soon as you receive notice that you are being downsized, apply for unemployment benefits online by visiting your state's official unemployment website. This information can be found through a simple web search or by visiting the US Department of Labor's website. You'll need to create an online account. Have your personal information handy, such as your Social Security number, driver's license, and employment history. It's crucial to provide accurate and complete information to avoid delays in processing your claim.*

Many individuals wait until their unemployment benefits expire (or close to it) before they start looking for work. I don't recommend waiting to begin the job search process, no matter what the reason. In today's job market, individuals are surprised and often shocked as to how long and how much work the job search process has become.

Chapter 3:

Get Organized: Your Job Search Toolkit

"All hard work brings a profit, but mere talk leads only to poverty."

Proverbs 14:23 (NIV)

The job search process can be a deeply personal and sometimes spiritual journey. It involves not only the practical steps of updating resumes and attending interviews but also the internal process of self-reflection and seeking guidance. For many, integrating prayer into this journey is a way to align their efforts with their faith, seeking wisdom and support beyond their own capabilities. This approach emphasizes the importance of the present moment and the power of incremental progress. Each small step, guided by prayer and reflection, contributes to the larger goal. Sharing one's burdens and challenges with others can also provide comfort and create a sense of community and shared purpose. This holistic approach to job searching can transform the experience from one of stress and uncertainty to one of growth, community, and faith-led purpose.

Organization is a learned skill. And as with any other new skill we are attempting to obtain or learn in our lives, it takes time and practice. A huge part of being organized is becoming "neat." To be able to find items around your desk when you need them is not only a sign of an organized person but is also more efficient. Start with something small—a stack of papers, mail that has piled up, or making sure there are no dishes piled up in the sink at any time. Start with small attention to details and you'll soon see how these small projects can expand to other areas of your life to create harmony and order. You'll start to feel better with these small accomplishments and, over time, will want to accomplish more.

Get Organized: Your Job Search Toolkit

Organize your job search path to success. Small action steps taken daily with a written action or goal plan will help you experience compounding results. Once you commit your strategies to paper, it will help you maintain focus toward your goal. It is vital, as with any management project, to have a written, detailed action plan.

Success comes from having or developing good habits, which ultimately help you create opportunities. God will give you clarity—if you ask Him for it—with your dreams and seeing your dreams come true. Prepare and plan for a higher level of living. Take action right where you are today, no matter how small the step.

HR departments use a job application software package called "Applicant Tracking System," otherwise known as ATS. When a person applies for a job at a company, the cover letter and resume go through this software, looking for a match in the "keywords" between your cover letter, resume, and the company job description. If there is no match between your cover letter, resume, and the job description, your application will automatically be moved into what I refer to as the "no" pile.

I'll use my own career and experience as an example of how the Applicant Tracking System works. As an HR benefits professional, I may list on my cover letter and resume my experience with "retirement" plans. If the job I'm applying for specifically refers to "experience with 401k or pension plans preferred" and I don't specifically list the keywords "401k or pension plans" on my cover letter and resume, the computer system will bypass my paperwork. In other words, my resume will never make it into the hands of the recruiter.

As computers get more and more sophisticated, they don't know how to think. At least not yet, anyway. The HR computer software systems do not know the words "retirement plans," "401k," or "pension plans" are all related. The software system is programmed to pick up certain terminology from your job application and run it up against the job description. If there is no match—no matter how qualified you may be for the position—your cover letter and resume are skipped over. How disappointing it may be to the job applicant when they read a job description and have determined it is a perfect fit! It meets all your job search criteria…You apply for the job and other similar jobs in your field, and the frustration that comes along with never receiving a response starts to rise. When that happens, that is because your application is missing one of two things: (1) a cover letter or (2) keywords in your cover letter and resume.

Many individuals complain as to the high number of job applications submitted versus the number of employer responses received. The reason for the discrepancy in employer responses is due to the lack of keywords used in the applicant's cover letter and resume. Keywords are found in the employer's job description.

A cover letter is vital to every job application as it is an opportunity to share "your story" and to introduce yourself to a prospective employer. It is your opportunity to share your strengths, talents, and experience and highlight what contributions you could bring to the employer or company. Most importantly, it is a tool for you to use and sell yourself—convince the prospective employer that you are perfect for the job position posted.

Employers are looking to see proof of accomplishments, and those accomplishments are outlined in your resume. Keep your resume less than two pages in length. When an HR recruiter reads your resume, they take an average of eight seconds (yes, eight seconds, not eight minutes) to review your resume and determine whether or not they are interested enough in scheduling a phone screening or interview. Basically, the top third portion of page one of your resume is reviewed with your most recent experience. The top third portion of your resume is what is known as "prime real estate." The information you include in that section of your resume—most importantly—will determine whether the recruiter remains interested enough in your resume to read further or place you in the "call-back" file.

Your contact information should be listed at the top of the page, including a professional summary. The professional summary (limit to one or two sentences) briefly explains to the recruiter your experience and what you are looking for. Be sure to include your name on the top of the resume. It is not necessary to include your home address. It is very important to include your email address, your LinkedIn address, and a contact phone number.

Please know that as a professional in today's job market, it is very important to have a presence—an account—on LinkedIn. Many recruiters will review your profile on LinkedIn after your resume has been vetted through the Applicant Tracking System. *Warning:* If you don't have an account on LinkedIn, chances are you will not be contacted by recruiters or staffing agencies. If they don't know you exist, how can you be contacted for a job?

I have met numerous individuals who are against having a LinkedIn account or are not interested in going through the process of setting up an account. I've been told it's "too much work." After hearing that, I think to myself, *These individuals are not interested in working again if they are not on the largest professional platform.*

A phone screening is different than a job interview; however, just as important. The initial phone screening made by a recruiter is normally a shorter version of an interview asking questions about your background, experience, and why you are interested in this position. Depending on how well you do with the phone screening process will determine whether you make it to the next step, which may be a Zoom or in-person interview.

Taking initiative on a project is great to place in your cover letter and mention during your phone screening or during your job interview. Be sure to talk about any money you saved for the company or dollar amount you saved previous employers. Dollar amounts saved are an attention grabber. Also, in your cover letter and in your resume, list any special awards or recognitions you received during your career. Today, employers are searching for individuals who can contribute to the success of the company and add value. Employers are not looking for someone who just wants to take up space or "float" until retirement. In other words, employers are looking to hire individuals who are "engaged" in their work.

Resumes should never be more than two pages in length. Avoid the term "references upon request" at the bottom of your resume, as it is an outdated term. Recruiters know that they can ask you for job references. No need to place it on your resume.

During the time you are unemployed, think about what is important to you. Once you've completed your list of job goals, remember to remain flexible during the job search process. Chances are you won't get 100 percent of what you are looking for; however, if you get 80 percent, you are doing quite well.

As you are going through your job search process and before you go on any interview, decide what is important to you. Here are a few examples:

- Know the salary range for your position. To find out this information, go to www.salary.com, or Google this information. Search by job title and zip code.

- What are your financial requirements? How much do you need to earn? How much experience do you have? What are you willing to accept? What are you comfortable accepting as far as a salary?

- Once you have this information, you are one step closer to being better equipped to negotiate and handle this question during the interview process.

- Are you willing to commute?

- Is it a hybrid position—working from home a few days a week while working in the office the other days? Or is it a full-time in-office position?

- What is my work-life balance like?

- If you are willing to commute, how long of a commute would you be satisfied with? How far are you willing to commute?

- Are benefits important to you? If yes, which ones?

- What hours are you willing to work?

- Is travel required as part of my job?

Prior to any job interview, and especially during the job search process, it is important to think about and determine your priorities. By deciding ahead of time what is important to you in your life, you are better prepared for your job search. You can then more easily identify opportunities that fit and align with your goals and values rather than aimlessly applying for any job.

By having a thought-out plan and determining what is important to you, not only are you setting boundaries as to what you would like in life and setting goals along with those boundaries, you are giving yourself self-respect. You respect yourself enough that you are thinking about the things that are important to you, rather than running an unstructured and unplanned job search process. You and God are a majority, and there is work to do on your end. You need to give God something to work with. You cannot expect to pray and sit back and watch Netflix all day. It takes work, in today's economy, to find a job. Yes, it is hard work, and it's not like the job search process we are used to seeing in the past. It's different today and different than two, three, or even five years ago. COVID did not change the job search process. The job application and job search process started to change about ten or so years ago.

Be prepared for your interview. If you are prepared, you are perceived as being informed and prepared. The assumption is that you would work the same way on the job.

It is also important to remain flexible during your job search process. Your next job may not be the job of a lifetime, but it may provide an opportunity for you to learn additional skills for a future, more advanced position.

Project an enthusiastic, engaging, energetic personality at all times. Make a concerted effort to be optimistic. That will also help you override any negative feelings you may have. Anticipate positive outcomes. Practice positive self-talk. Focus on your successes. Keep smiling. Associate with positive people and avoid negative ones.

Here are a few questions to ask yourself to find out what is important to you for your next job or career:

- Are you looking for the same job you had before?
- Are you interested in a career change?
- Would you like to work less hours?
- Would you like more or less responsibility?

The job market is dynamic and often requires individuals to adapt to new trends and technologies. Lifelong learning is a crucial aspect of maintaining employability, as it allows individuals to stay current with evolving industry standards and practices. For those who have been out of work, it's essential to approach the job search with flexibility and a willingness to learn. This includes being open to updating one's resume, acquiring new skills, and even changing industries if necessary. The willingness to adapt can significantly shorten the duration of unemployment. Moreover, the job search process itself has changed, with digital platforms becoming the norm for finding opportunities and networking. Understanding these changes and leveraging them can be the key to re-entering the workforce successfully. It's also important to utilize available resources, such as career counseling or workshops, which can provide guidance and improve one's chances of finding employment.

The omission of a cover letter with job applications is a significant oversight. A cover letter provides a critical opportunity for a candidate to personalize their application and highlight how their unique skills and experiences align with the role's requirements. It's a chance to make a compelling case for why they are the best fit for the position, going beyond the resume to tell a story that engages the hiring manager. Without it, applicants miss the chance to stand out in a competitive job market, where a personalized approach can make all the difference. Crafting a tailored cover letter for each application demonstrates professionalism, attention to detail, and a genuine interest in the role, which are qualities highly valued by employers. If you do not take the time to tailor your cover letter and resume for the position you are applying for, this would be considered "a lost opportunity." Submitting a resume without a cover letter is a lost opportunity to "tell and sell" your story to a prospective employer or recruiter.

Leveraging the resources available through unemployment offices, such as job counseling and training classes, is a strategic move for job seekers. These programs are designed to enhance employability by updating skills and providing knowledge that is crucial in the current job market. For instance, mastering Microsoft Office applications can significantly improve job prospects, as these are fundamental tools in many industries. Furthermore, specialized workshops like "How to Ace Your Job Interviews" and "Resume Writing" offer invaluable insights that can give candidates a competitive edge. Embracing the concept of lifelong learning not only keeps skills relevant but also demonstrates a proactive attitude to potential employers. Engaging in these opportunities can shorten the duration of unemployment and lead to more fulfilling career paths.

Embracing new learning opportunities, whether re-entering the job market, making a career change, graduating from college, or facing unemployment, can be a crucial step toward personal and professional development. The mindset of continuous learning and improvement is often what sets apart successful job seekers. It's not just about writing a resume; it's about understanding the nuances of how resumes are evolving, the importance of keywords for applicant tracking systems, and the best ways to showcase one's skills and experiences. Moreover, classes like these offer networking opportunities, a chance to exchange ideas with peers, and a structured environment to stay motivated. It's understandable to feel overwhelmed or disheartened during job transitions, but remaining open to growth and new knowledge can indeed be a game-changer in today's dynamic job market.

The duration of unemployment can indeed be influenced by an individual's adaptability and willingness to learn. The job market is dynamic and affected by various factors such as economic conditions, technological advancements, and global competition. Research indicates that during economic downturns, unemployment durations can increase significantly. Additionally, the rise of automation and the need for new skill sets can make it challenging for those who are not open to learning and change. Lifelong learning is essential in this context, as it allows individuals to stay relevant and competitive in the job market. Embracing a mindset of continuous personal and professional development can be a decisive factor in shortening the period of unemployment and securing new opportunities.

Joining professional associations is a strategic move for career growth and professional development. These organizations offer a wealth of resources, including support from peers, insights into industry trends, and opportunities for referrals. Networking within these groups can significantly increase your visibility in the field, opening doors to various opportunities and events. It's essential to have a system to organize the numerous contacts you'll make; efficient contact management ensures you can follow up and connect with them on platforms like LinkedIn. This not only helps in maintaining professional relationships but also in leveraging these connections for potential collaborations or job prospects. Remember, the key to effective networking is not just in making new contacts but in nurturing those connections over time.

Networking, when done effectively, is about forging genuine connections that are mutually beneficial. It's an art of building relationships where the focus is not on what you can gain but on what you can offer. At a networking event, for instance, a person might engage in conversations that are not just about exchanging business cards but about sharing knowledge, offering support, and understanding the challenges others face. By motivating others and helping to elevate their mood, you contribute to a positive atmosphere that encourages collaboration and trust. This approach not only enriches the professional community but also fosters a network where everyone feels valued and supported.

Lifelong learning is not a trend but a keyword that employers are looking for in today's job candidates. Throughout your entire career, skill set improvements, certifications, classes, and in short, continued learning is the key. Be open to new ideas. Be open to consistent and constant learning. Take an active role in your learning. Counteract any negative self-talk by changing your inner voice to one that is more uplifting and positive. Change what you are saying to yourself. Do not berate yourself or put yourself down. Learn from your experience. As part of your own self-care, be kind to yourself. Although we all strive to be better in our lives, to our loved ones, and in our careers, no one is perfect. Don't beat yourself up because you did not get that job. You prepared well for the interview, and then the company decided to cut its budget. Make an attempt not to take it personally when you did not get the job you were really after. Take time to think about what you could have done better, learn from the experience, and move on. Perhaps it's learning new skills so that you remain competitive in the job market.

To find relevant courses for lifelong learning, you can explore various online platforms that offer a wide range of subjects and skills to enhance your professional and personal development. For instance, Coursera provides a course designed to help you adopt a growth mindset and develop critical thinking and problem-solving skills. Harvard University offers a comprehensive catalog of courses for professionals, distance learners, and those seeking higher learning in retirement. Additionally, websites like Class Central list online courses from top universities worldwide, allowing you to earn certificates in lifelong learning. Platforms such as edX, Udemy, and others also offer courses from universities and colleges globally, covering countless subjects to match your interests and career goals. It's essential to evaluate these platforms based on the quality of content, the expertise of instructors, and the flexibility of the learning schedule to ensure they meet your needs for continuous education and skill enhancement. In addition, there are many free courses online, and LinkedIn offers an array of online courses for a monthly fee. It's worth the investment to take LinkedIn classes, as they will be posted on your profile upon completion.

The job search process is indeed a job in itself, requiring a strategic approach akin to navigation. Crafting a detailed plan, akin to a GPS, can streamline the path to potential employment opportunities. A thorough investigation of each prospective employer is crucial. Scrutinizing the composition and experience of a company's Board of Directors can offer insights into its governance and diversity, which are key indicators of a company's culture and values. Reflecting on personal achievements and contributions to previous roles is equally important. Quantifiable accomplishments, such as cost-saving measures, process improvements, leadership roles, or awards, are compelling evidence of one's potential value to a new employer. In today's competitive job market, employers are on the lookout for candidates who not only fulfill the job requirements but also bring fresh ideas and energy to the table, thereby contributing to the company's growth and innovation.

Conducting thorough research on a potential employer is a critical step in the job application process. It demonstrates your genuine interest in the position and the company, and it provides valuable insights that can be leveraged during an interview. By understanding the company's current projects, financial health, and strategic direction, you can tailor your responses to align with its objectives and culture. Documenting your findings not only helps you stay organized but also prepares you to ask informed questions, showing your proactive approach. Evaluating whether the company's growth trajectory and future plans resonate with your career aspirations ensures that the opportunity is a good fit for both parties. Ultimately, this level of preparation can set you apart as a candidate who is not only well-informed but also deeply invested in contributing to the company's success.

Effective interview preparation involves a strategic approach to communication and organization. Crafting concise, targeted responses to potential questions can demonstrate clarity of thought and respect for the interviewer's time. Practicing delivery in front of a mirror can help refine non-verbal cues and build confidence. Embracing moments of silence rather than filling them with nervous chatter allows for thoughtful reflection and can convey composure. Remembering to write down key points, tasks, and questions ensures that nothing important is overlooked during the job search process. For virtual interviews, such as those conducted via Zoom or Teams, the setting plays a crucial role. A professional, distraction-free background can make a positive impression and signal attention to detail. It's these nuances that can distinguish a candidate and make a memorable impact during the interview process. When it comes to interview questions, it's important to reflect positively on your experiences. For instance, if asked why you stayed at a company for an extended period, you might discuss the valuable experience gained, the growth opportunities that were available, or the strong relationships built with colleagues. Similarly, when discussing what you enjoyed about working for a past employer, focus on the positive aspects, such as the company culture, the mission, or the professional development it offered. Always remember to present both yourself and your former employer in the best possible light, regardless of any negative experiences, as this reflects your professionalism and ability to handle challenging situations gracefully.

In the professional world, maintaining a positive image of your former employer is crucial. Speaking ill of past experiences can reflect poorly on your character and professionalism. It's essential to control non-verbal cues, as body language can convey much more than words, especially in virtual meetings where visual cues are significant. Smiling can project confidence and approachability. The setting of your video interview is also vital; a neutral, organized background can prevent distractions and convey a professional atmosphere. A bookcase or a simple, uncluttered space can be ideal. Avoiding overly personal or casual backdrops is wise, as it helps maintain the focus on your professional attributes. Remember, simplicity in your background can help ensure that the attention remains on you and your qualifications.

First impressions are crucial in an interview setting, where every detail can convey a message about your professionalism and suitability for the role. A well-organized and tidy background suggests thoroughness and attention to detail, while a cluttered or distracting background might raise questions about your work habits. Being prepared with well-thought-out interview questions demonstrates your interest in the position and your proactive approach. Behavioral interview questions offer a chance to showcase your problem-solving skills and how you handle various situations, essentially allowing you to narrate your professional journey. Remember, a genuine smile can set a positive tone for the interaction, making you appear approachable and confident.

Accomplishments and overcoming challenges are pivotal aspects of personal and professional growth. For instance, an individual might consider completing a complex project under a tight deadline an accomplishment or successfully navigating a career transition as overcoming a challenge. Learning from these experiences often involves gaining new skills, such as time management or adaptability, and applying them to future situations. Continuous improvement on the job can be achieved through various means, such as seeking feedback, setting personal benchmarks, and pursuing ongoing education or training. The last class one might have taken could be related to their field or an area of interest, like a course in advanced data analysis or a workshop on leadership skills.

HR insider tip. Creating a dedicated workspace at home is crucial for a focused and effective job search. This is your "new office," and the space should be quiet, organized, and separate from the daily distractions of home life. It's important to have all the necessary tools at hand, such as a laptop, a reliable internet connection, a printer, and any other resources that might be needed during the job search process. Privacy is key, especially for conducting phone or video interviews where confidentiality and professionalism are paramount. While coffee shops like Starbucks and Dunkin' can offer a change of scenery and networking opportunities, they often lack the controlled environment needed for sustained concentration and productivity. A consistent, well-equipped space at home will provide the best setting for a successful job search.

Chapter 4:

Your New Day Job

"Through idleness of the hands the house leaks."

Ecclesiastes 10:18 (NKJV)

The wisdom from Ecclesiastes about idleness leading to a metaphorical "leaking house" is timeless. It suggests that without purposeful action, things tend to fall into disrepair, which can be applied to many aspects of life, including managing one's time effectively. Creating a structured plan for your job search is a proactive step toward productivity. It could involve setting specific goals, breaking them down into manageable tasks, and allocating time slots for each activity, whether it's job searching, skill development, or leisure. Prioritizing tasks and setting clear objectives for each day can help in making the most of one's time, ensuring that, at the end of the day, there's a sense of accomplishment and progress. Remember, every small step counts, and consistency is key to turning plans into action.

Creating a structured plan is indeed a proactive step towards productivity, especially during unemployment. It's important to establish a routine that includes dedicated time for job searching, skill development, and personal projects. Setting specific goals for each day can help maintain focus and momentum. For instance, mornings could be allocated for job applications, afternoons for learning new skills or freelancing, and evenings for networking or leisure activities that also contribute to well-being. It's also beneficial to set measurable objectives, like applying to a certain number of jobs per week, completing a course or certification, or building a portfolio. Additionally, incorporating physical exercise and social interactions into the daily schedule can greatly improve mental health and provide a sense of balance. Remember, productivity isn't just about work; it's about making progress in various aspects of life. By having a clear plan, it's easier to track progress, stay motivated, and ultimately transition into a new role with confidence and a broadened skill set.

Your New Day Job

Approaching the job search process is similar to approaching a home renovation, which can be overwhelming without a clear plan. Just like in home improvement, where one might decide to tackle the bathroom first, ensuring all the plumbing is in order before moving on to painting the bedrooms, a job search requires a similar strategy. It's about setting priorities, understanding the steps involved, and methodically moving through them. For instance, one might start by updating their resume before diving into the job market, ensuring it reflects their skills and experiences accurately. Then, they might focus on networking, reaching out to contacts, and attending industry events. Following that, they could concentrate on applying to jobs that align with their career goals and preparing for interviews. Each step is like a room in the house, requiring attention and care before moving on to the next. And just as one would budget for home renovations, it's crucial to allocate time and resources effectively during a job hunt. This might mean setting aside specific hours each day for job-related activities or investing in courses to enhance one's skills. Ultimately, whether it's fixing up a home or finding a new job, the key is to have a plan, set realistic goals, and take it one step at a time, ensuring progress is made and efforts are concentrated where they matter most. This methodical approach not only helps manage resources better but also brings a sense of accomplishment as one completes each phase, be it a freshly painted room or a successful job interview.

Creating a dedicated job search space is a crucial step in establishing a productive and organized approach to finding new employment opportunities. This space should be quiet, well-lit, and equipped with all the necessary supplies, such as a computer, a reliable internet connection, notepads, pens, and a calendar for scheduling follow-ups and interviews. It's important to treat your home office—your work area—as a professional workspace, which means minimizing distractions and setting clear boundaries to maintain focus. Personalizing the space with items that inspire motivation can also help in maintaining a positive mindset throughout the job search process. Remember, consistency in your environment can lead to consistency in your efforts and results.

In today's fast-paced job market, being proactive and prepared is crucial. It's essential to stay current with industry trends and skills. In the case of job loss, it's advisable to immediately apply for unemployment benefits and begin the job search process without delay. Investing in a laptop is a positive step, as it's a vital tool for job searching and skill development. However, it's just the beginning; creating a structured job search plan, updating one's resume, and actively applying for positions are equally important steps to regain employment. Being prepared and taking action promptly can significantly reduce the duration of unemployment and increase the chances of finding a suitable new role.

Your New Day Job

Navigating the job market after a layoff can indeed be a challenging experience, especially for individuals over the age of fifty. The duration of unemployment can vary greatly, often influenced by factors such as industry demand, job level, and the individual's professional network. While a severance package can provide temporary financial relief, it's important to consider the long-term implications of a career gap. Proactive job searching, upskilling, and networking are crucial steps in this transitional phase. It's also beneficial to explore resources such as career counseling, job fairs, and professional workshops that can provide support and increase job prospects. Taking time to recharge is understandable, but maintaining a balance and staying active in the job market can lead to more fruitful opportunities.

Losing a job can indeed be a distressing experience, and it's natural to feel a range of emotions, including anger and confusion. It's important to acknowledge these feelings but also to move forward proactively. The job market has evolved significantly, with new technologies and networking platforms transforming how job searches are conducted. Today, a successful job search strategy involves a strong online presence, leveraging professional networks, and continuous skill development. It's essential to approach this process with determination and resilience, viewing it as an opportunity for growth and new beginnings. Remember, every setback can lead to new pathways and possibilities.

Navigating the modern job search landscape requires a strategic approach, and indeed, perseverance is a key component of any successful career plan. The concept of taking "baby steps" is a practical method to manage the overwhelming nature of job hunting and career progression. It allows for a focused approach to each task, making the process more manageable and less daunting. By concentrating on the present, one can maintain a sense of control and progress incrementally towards their goals.

Concerns about financial obligations such as severance, car payments, mortgages, and retirement are legitimate and can cause significant stress. However, by breaking down these concerns into smaller, actionable steps, they become more manageable. For instance, creating a budget can help in tracking expenses and savings, while exploring alternative income sources can provide additional financial security. Networking, upskilling, and staying informed about industry trends are also crucial steps in enhancing employability and job security.

Moreover, it's important to recognize the value of adaptability in today's dynamic job market. Embracing change and being open to new opportunities can lead to unexpected and rewarding career paths. Mental and emotional well-being is equally important; practicing mindfulness and self-care can help in maintaining a positive outlook during challenging times.

The journey of career advancement and career satisfaction

is unique to each individual, and what works for one may not work for another. It's about finding a balance between planning for the future and living in the present, between being proactive and patient. As the adage suggests, placing one foot in front of the other, one step at a time, is a wise approach to not only career development but life in general. It's a reminder that progress, no matter how small, is still progress.

In the current job market, the ability to adapt and apply one's skills to new contexts is crucial. Continuous learning, as you've practiced throughout your career, not only enriches your professional toolkit but also demonstrates a proactive and resilient mindset to potential employers. Networking, both online and in-person, can uncover opportunities that align with your career aspirations and values. Engaging with professional communities, attending industry events, and connecting with peers can lead to discovering roles that value your specialized knowledge and offer a fulfilling career trajectory.

As you navigate this transition, consider the core competencies that have underpinned your success, such as strategic thinking and an understanding of organizational dynamics—and how these can be your greatest assets in a new role. Reflect on the aspects of your work that you most enjoy and excel at, and seek out positions that emphasize these elements. With a clear vision of your strengths and a willingness to embrace new challenges, the next chapter of your professional journey can be as rewarding as the last.

Now, how do you get organized, especially if you were not a person who was very organized previously? It's a mindset; it's a habit. Again, something new to learn. The journey through unemployment and the quest for a new job can indeed be a profound period of self-discovery and personal growth. It's a time when one's resilience is tested, and the true colors of relationships often come to light. The process can be isolating, as the intense personal investment in the job search is not always matched by those around us. This disparity can lead to revelations about the nature of friendships and the support one can expect from their social circle. It's not uncommon to find that empathy has its limits, and actions—or the lack thereof—can speak louder than words. The experience of reaching out for help and being met with reluctance or refusal can be disheartening, but it can also serve as a catalyst for reevaluating relationships and recognizing the value of reciprocal support.

The journey of personal growth and achievement is often hindered by the presence of negative influences, whether they be habits or individuals. These negative elements act as obstacles, subtly eroding the foundation of our aspirations and dreams. Over time, their impact can accumulate, leading to a significant diversion from one's intended path. The realization of this can be disheartening as one reflects on the dreams that remain unrealized and the goals that seem increasingly unattainable.

However, it is within the power of each individual to initiate change. By stepping back and reassessing one's current trajectory, it becomes possible to identify the negative influences that need to be addressed. Proactivity is the key to altering one's course toward a more desirable future. It is a call to action, urging one not to become a bystander in their own life, watching as potential remains untapped and aspirations go unfulfilled.

The responsibility for this transformation lies squarely on the shoulders of the individual. It is a personal duty to become cognizant of the factors that shape one's life and to take deliberate steps toward improvement. This process often requires a shift in daily habits, aligning them with the vision of the life one yearns to lead. The challenge lies in bridging the gap between dreaming of a different life and actualizing it.

Many find themselves trapped in a cycle of routine, yearning for change but uncertain of the path to take. The key realization is that if one desires a different outcome, the impetus for change must come from within. It is a recognition that the power to alter one's destiny is self-contained. The phrase "If it is to be, it is up to me" encapsulates this ethos, emphasizing the role of personal agency in effecting change.

Deciding not to act is, in itself, a choice that shapes one's future. What one experiences today is the result of past decisions, and what one will experience tomorrow hinges on the choices made in the present. If one seeks transformation, it must begin with a commitment to personal change. This is the essence of self-empowerment, the understanding that, for anything to change, it must start with oneself.

The journey to self-improvement and achieving one's dreams is indeed a personal and challenging endeavor. It begins with the recognition that each day is a finite resource, and how one chooses to allocate their time and energy can significantly influence their life's trajectory. The process of introspection is crucial; it involves examining one's habits, behaviors, and the company one keeps. Identifying and altering detrimental habits is a formidable task, often because these patterns are deeply ingrained and offer a deceptive sense of comfort. Yet, it is essential to acknowledge that such habits—be it an unhealthy diet, sedentary lifestyle, or unmanaged stress—can impede progress toward personal goals.

Cultivating new, positive habits and surrounding oneself with supportive individuals can create an environment conducive to growth. It's about making conscious choices, setting realistic goals, and taking consistent, purposeful actions. The transformation from passive wishing to active striving is what bridges the gap between the current self and the envisioned future. It's a path marked by small victories and inevitable setbacks, but persistence and resilience can lead to profound change.

Moreover, the struggle against bad habits is not a solitary fight. Seeking guidance, whether through literature, mentorship, or professional help, can provide the strategies and support needed to overcome these challenges. It's also important to celebrate progress, no matter how small, as it reinforces the positive changes and motivates one to continue.

Ultimately, the realization that the key to unlocking one's potential lies within is empowering. It shifts the focus from external circumstances to internal strength and accountability. By embracing this mindset, individuals can begin to take control of their habits, their time, and their lives, moving steadily toward the life they aspire to lead. The transformation is gradual, the journey is ongoing, and the outcomes are as unique as the individuals themselves. But the common thread is the belief that change is possible, and it starts with the decision to take action. It's also important to celebrate progress, no matter how small, as it reinforces the positive changes and motivates one to continue.

Bad habits hold us back in areas that we desire to change:

- Wealth
- Health
- Happiness
- Love or meaningful human connection
- Self-confidence
- Self-esteem.

Overcoming bad habits is a journey that begins with self-awareness and a commitment to change. The areas of wealth, health, happiness, love, self-confidence, and self-esteem are interconnected facets of life where improvement can lead to a more fulfilling existence. The process of change is not instantaneous; it requires a structured approach, starting with clear goal-setting.

The act of purchasing a notebook and pens is symbolic of the readiness to commit thoughts to paper, which is a powerful step toward materializing one's aspirations. Writing down goals is not just about recording them; it's about clarifying and giving them form. This clarity is crucial because it transforms vague desires into actionable objectives.

Once goals are set, the next step is to outline the specific actions required to achieve them. This could involve breaking down larger goals into smaller, manageable tasks, setting deadlines, and identifying resources and support systems. It's also important to anticipate potential obstacles and plan for how to address them.

Regularly reviewing and adjusting the plan is essential, as progress might reveal new insights or necessitate changes in strategy. Celebrating small victories along the way can provide motivation and reinforce the habit of persistence.

Moreover, developing a plan is not just about reaching an end goal; it's about cultivating the discipline and habits that lead to sustained success. This might include establishing routines, seeking knowledge and advice, and learning from both successes and failures.

Get your supplies in order for your new career and stick to your "success plan." Instead of thinking about all that you have to do, it starts with a simple step of writing it down.

Did you know that having everything in your head without writing it down causes stress? The act of writing down your goals alleviates 50 percent of your stress as they are out of your head and onto a piece of paper. When all the "things" that you need to do are running around in your brain, you tend to get overwhelmed. Then, we lose sleep at night, thinking about what we need to do. The act of writing down your goals and the steps needed for the completion of a successful job search is actually a destresser. It takes the pressure of trying to remember everything and getting it out of your head and onto paper—where you can then see it.

Writing down your goals and seeing them on paper also increases your success rate in attaining them. Studies have shown that it takes the pressure off of your brain of rehashing what you need to do over and over again. It also helps you be "in the moment" with your family and other tasks that you need to accomplish in your life. It reduces the "preoccupied" moments and helps you focus. Once you have completed your job search accomplishments for the day, you can then enjoy the rest of your day. Go for a walk, get some fresh air, or go to the gym. Relax, have confidence that God hears your prayers, and He will get you the right job at the right time.

Because bad habits are stored in your subconscious mind and are "automatic responses," it will take some work to notice or question what you are doing. The key is to become more mindful. Many of us don't think about what we are doing as we are going through automatic responses. Some of us are just going through the motions. Whether your goal is personal health, retirement, savings, a new car, or vacation, bad habits slow us down. Bad habits also use up our resources if our habits are not in alignment with our goals. My recommendation for turning a bad habit into a good one is to find something more constructive or more interesting to do with your time.

Once you decide to change your bad habits, you will find your life moving in a positive direction. However, these changes will not happen overnight. Instead of being negative and destructive, you will feel yourself becoming more positive and productive.

Reflecting on what you would like to change in your life is a challenging process that involves self-awareness and patience. It involves prayer, wisdom, and guidance from the Holy Spirit. Perhaps you would like to make a career change that aligns more with your passions, or you would prefer more work-life balance. Writing down and acknowledging the habits you wish to change is a powerful first step in contributing to a healthier, happier life.

Keep in mind: good habits (not the bad ones) are the habits that will help you get to your long-term goals. Keeping track of your progress makes a huge difference. Once you have made a list of goals to accomplish put a date on the top of the page to track your accomplishments.

As the week progresses and you are busy accomplishing your goals, check them off with a different colored pen to make them stand out. For example, if one of your goals was to sign up for a free class at your local library or through your state's unemployment office, and you enrolled, check off that goal. Put a line through that goal, and next to it write the word, "Victory!" When you see the goal completed, it provides a huge sense of accomplishment. Completing that process actually encourages you—

to do more and go after your goals. It's turning a part of your job search process into a game, with the reward being the check mark. You are encouraging yourself with what you have accomplished. At the end of the day or the end of the week, you can see how many items you have checkmarked off your list.

The American Journal of Psychology defines a "habit" as a fixed way of thinking or feeling that was acquired through a previous experience. The behavioral patterns of habits become hard to break; however, through awareness, mindfulness, practice, and repetition, new habits can form and replace bad ones.

We are not trapped into bad habits or wrong ways of thinking. Habits become more difficult to change, especially if it is a bad habit we have had for a long time. Become more self-aware, identify which bad habits you have that are not working for you. This discovery process could be made during meditation or any quiet prayer time you have set aside during the day. Ask God to help you identify your bad habits and ask Him help in learning new and better ways to live. God wants you to live a fuller life and He loves when you go to Him in prayer. God promises in His Word to help you.

Do we use our time on habits that make us feel hopeless, unhealthy, and alone? Or do we focus and do the work to promote health, a better financial future, and a life full of meaningful relationships? What type of life do we choose?

All habits require action. Are your actions or choices contributing to your goals or moving you further away from your goals? You may discover that you have some habits that are not so good and require changing. You may not feel happy or good when you need to change an old habit. Over time, your new habits that will assist you in moving you toward the goals and dreams you have set for your life will eventually feel enjoyable. However, this all takes time, work, and mindfulness.

Are you willing to do the work to accomplish your goals and dreams to live the life you have always imagined or dreamed for yourself? Isn't it about time to get down to the business of creating and living your dream life instead of wondering why it hasn't happened yet or wondering why it hasn't magically appeared?

Change is hard and most people avoid change as it is perceived as a bad thing. The best way to make change stick is to replace a bad habit with a positive habit. When you think negatively, you then act negatively. When you think positively, your actions will be positive. If you are critical with yourself, you will feel bad about yourself, which is a major block for success in your life.

Bad habits could have started decades back, and you may require professional help to discover how and why you started them in the first place. Keep your eye on the goal and ask God to help you.

"What the mind can conceive and believe it can achieve." Your brain is the original super-computer. Limiting beliefs in ourselves keeps us stuck. The best way to combat limiting beliefs is by transforming your mind with the Word of God. The Bible is a book written with a focus on "renewing" your mind and getting you to think differently about yourself, your life, and your life's purpose.

Dream big and set goals. Not setting any goals for yourself has negative consequences, as it affects your self-esteem. It is an indirect way of putting yourself down, as you don't think you are important enough or worth it to take action on your goals. *Setting goals makes you happy.*

Start small and take a look around the workspace you have designated for your job search. Look around. Is it cluttered? Is there a coffee cup or two around that should be placed in the dishwasher? Is there a tower of paper or books piled up in a corner? Take a few minutes—say ten to twenty minutes a day—to keep your workspace, home, and car clutter-free. You'll be surprised by the end of the week how much you have accomplished. A clean and organized home office environment keeps your mind focused as it is not distracted by the clutter and chaos around you. A cluttered house, car, workspace, or office results in a cluttered mind. With a cluttered mind, you are unable to concentrate or focus on your job search. You will find yourself distracted by the clutter around you.

If you are unable to find anything you need during your job search process, that is a time waster. Place items in their proper place. Then, you'll be able to put your hands on the items you need when you need them. Nothing wastes more time than searching for an item that you know you have—somewhere—and you can't find it. It's frustrating and not productive. Changing your environment to an organized and clutter-free zone creates a stress-free environment.

Maintain your physical and mental health while looking for work. Happiness comes from your mind, from what you think. Be mindful of how you think and how you feel inside. Work on eliminating bad habits. Every step you take in life is either building what you want or moving away from your goals.

Habits are a routine. The more you do them, the harder they are to break. Identify any habits that keep you from living the best life you can, now. Make your life a priority by making time for yourself. Pouring all your energy into caring for others and not leaving any time to care for yourself can burn you out. It is necessary to find time to recharge, find some alone time, and pray. Solitude is good for the soul.

Many of us don't have big dreams and goals. Develop a record of making good choices for yourself. This is how your confidence and esteem will grow. Bad habits will lower your confidence and self-esteem. Good habits will increase your self-esteem and self-confidence. Spend time every day to know yourself through meditation, prayer time, and alone time. Be a lifetime learner: gain more knowledge. To feel more confident, gain more knowledge. Become an expert in your field. If you need to make a career change, make a plan to get there as it doesn't happen overnight.

Follow through on your actions. If you don't intend to do something, then don't say you are going to do it; all talk and no action. Say what you mean, mean what you say, but don't say it mean.

Not doing what you said you would do is a habit that makes others think you can't be trusted. However, it also affects your self-esteem and makes you think you can't trust yourself.

Follow through on your words. Proverbs 18:21 (NIV) says, "The tongue has the power of life and death, and those who love it will eat its fruit."

If you follow up on what you say, you are showing yourself and others that you can be trusted and are a person of integrity. If you don't do what you say as a habit, it makes others think you can't be trusted. It also affects your self-esteem. It also makes you think that you can't trust yourself.

Spend quiet time with yourself. Learn what is important to you. Follow your dreams. Meditate, go for a walk, exercise, pick up a new hobby. Listen to your inner voice. Cultivate your inner voice. Prayer time and meditation are extremely helpful in getting to know yourself.

Watch over negative thoughts and don't let them overpower you. Take hold of your thoughts and believe in yourself. Work on your determination.

Treat everyone with respect. Never stop learning, listening to your instincts, and loving yourself. Self-care means making sure all parts of oneself are taken care of, not just physical needs but also mental and emotional as well.

Keep a clear vision of where you want to go. Develop a new habit of determining your goal and then making a plan.

HR insider tip. Beginning a job search is akin to starting a new project. It's essential to approach it with a structured plan and dedicated time commitment. Start with a clear understanding of your career goals and desired industry. Creating your personal mission statement helps in tailoring your job searches more effectively as it provides focus and direction. Remember: A well-organized job search strategy, along with a personal mission statement, an updated resume, and a cover letter that includes "keywords," can significantly increase your chances of success.

Chapter 5:

Activate Your Plan

"He becomes poor who works with a slack and idle hand, but the hand of the diligent makes rich."

Proverbs 10:4 (AMPCE)

The journey to success is a structured endeavor, much like a meticulously drafted map that guides a traveler to their destination. It begins with a vision, a clear and compelling picture of the desired outcome, which acts as the north star, guiding every step taken. This vision is then broken down into actionable objectives, forming the backbone of a strategic plan. The plan itself is a living document, adaptable and responsive to the ever-changing landscape of one's career path. It requires not just creation but activation, a deliberate and sustained effort to bring the words on paper to life through consistent action.

Each day becomes a series of intentional steps, marked on the calendar as non-negotiable appointments with one's future self. These steps are specific, measurable, and time-bound, ensuring that every action taken is a building block toward the ultimate goal. It's about harnessing the power of action, recognizing that each task completed is a ripple in the pond of progress, creating momentum that propels one forward. Visualization plays a key role in this process, serving as a mental rehearsal for success, where the mind's eye sees the achievement of goals long before they materialize in reality.

The Bible reinforces the truth that what one can conceive and believe, one can achieve. It speaks to the profound connection between the mental and the physical realms, where the act of seeing oneself in possession of their goals creates a bridge between desire and reality. This is the essence of faith in action, a dynamic interplay between belief and behavior, where the former inspires the latter, and together, they forge the path to success.

The creation of an action plan is not merely an exercise in organization but a declaration of intent. It is a commitment to oneself, a promise to pursue one's aspirations with vigor and resolve. It is an acknowledgment that while dreams are the seeds of reality, it is through the soil of hard work and the water of perseverance that they sprout and grow. Thus, the action plan becomes a sacred contract, a covenant with the future, where today's efforts are the currency with which tomorrow's achievements are purchased. And in this pursuit, action is indeed power, the catalyst that transforms the intangible into the tangible, the unseen into the seen, and the dream into the achievement.

Success is a journey that begins with the belief in oneself. It's about setting intentions and aligning actions with those intentions. By adopting a positive mindset geared toward success, a person's life can be transformed profoundly. Yes, it's about dreaming big, thinking big, and believing big. Focus on how big your God is and not on the size of your challenge or "mountains" in life. Obstacles are less significant when compared to the strength and magnitude of one's faith and God's support. Remember: Faith can move mountains.

Success is an inside job, a mindset, and it starts with a decision to change. The expectation of greater things in your life is the first step toward making them a reality. To have the confidence and knowledge to have a greater expectation starts with the renewing of your mind—that decision you made to change, which starts with renewing your mind through the Bible. The Bible is your blueprint, your "road map" to take you through this journey called life. Developing an expectation of positive results, you are taking intentional steps toward increased success in your life.

Here are some points to ponder about success that you might not have considered previously:

- Success is intentional and doesn't just "happen." The right thought process, the right thoughts combined with taking the right action, will guide you to success. If not, you will learn from the experience and make adjustments the next time.

- Success is a lifestyle and not a "one-and-done" experience. Success is consistent action taken in everything you do. Sounds like a lot of work because success is—work.

- Success equals action. We can all dream about success and visualize what it would be like, but ultimately, we need to act on our plan. Additional prayer time may be required if we are afraid to take the next step.

- Success requires thinking big. We serve a big God. He created the universe—the galaxies and beyond. Don't limit God with small thinking. Make a list and ask God for your dream life. Then, watch the miracles occur over time.

Activate Your Plan

The journey of your job search is within itself a journey of self-improvement. It begins when we recognize our unique talents and what drives us. It's about taking ownership of our lives, becoming proactive, and choosing to adopt a new perspective on ourselves and our capabilities. We then set the stage for success. This success is not just an outcome but a way of life that demands consistent action and the courage to dream, think, and believe. It's about setting expectations high and striving to meet them.

Remember that our thoughts shape our reality and our world. This emphasizes the importance of a positive mindset and proactive behavior in achieving personal excellence. Consistency in our efforts and quality of work reflects a commitment to our goals and aspirations. It's not only about exerting more effort but making sure we are moving our efforts in the right direction. Writing down a plan is a tangible step toward materializing our thoughts and giving them structure. Setting goals not only provides clarity but also directs our focus, acting as a compass guiding us through life's journey toward fulfilling our true potential and finding our unique place in the world.

The concept of thriving versus surviving is a powerful mindset shift. It's about transcending the day-to-day grind and finding fulfillment in what we do. Thriving involves seeking out and engaging in work that aligns with our passions and values, which in turn can lead to greater satisfaction and happiness. It's about crafting a life where our job is not just a means to an end but a source of joy and fulfillment. This holistic approach to living doesn't just benefit us on a personal level; it can radiate outwards, positively impacting those around us and the wider community. The Scripture from Job 22:28 encapsulates the idea that our intentions and declarations have power. By setting our sights on thriving, we can create a reality that is rich with purpose and joy. "Thou shall decree a thing, and it shall be established unto thee" (Job 22:28).

For example, instead of saying, "I want a job" or "I need a job," change it as follows:

> I want to obtain a (*list your desired job title here*) position with a (*small/medium/large company*) making *(list your desired salary requirements here*), close to home, with great health benefits, and with the option of working remotely. An environment where I can grow as a professional and learn new skills.

You can elaborate as you find necessary as to how this statement fits into your life and your goals.

Writing your own personal mission statement for yourself and your life will help you stay focused throughout your job search strategy. It will help keep you on track as it answers not only the "what" you are looking to do but the "why" behind it.

Activate Your Plan

It's a statement about who you are and what it is that you desire in your life. It helps your job search efforts by framing not only what you want to do in your life but also the "why." A personal mission statement helps put the power behind why you are conducting a job search. The personal mission statement helps you get motivated as you say to yourself, *Yes, I want this because...* A goal helps you focus on what you want and sets the course for the direction of your dreams.

After you decide on your "action plan statement," you are ready to put action behind the plan you developed for yourself. Put it to work. You are ready to move forward with more confidence and with an attitude of excellence. You now have a mission, and you know the direction of your plan. Your energy now knows to move in this direction.

Today is a new day and a gift from God. Every day is another opportunity to start anew. Trust God! Persistence is the number one personality trait that will get you through your job search and land your next career opportunity.

After defining your "mission" or "action plan statement," outline the goals and objectives of your job search, and then activate that plan. Defining your "action plan statement" is similar to programming your destination within a GPS. The GPS may be activated and a helpful tool; however, without directions or instructions, the technology is not useful. Similar to your job search. If you don't have a focus, apply for any or every job available, or work sporadically on your job search—you won't make any progress. You'll remain stuck in the same place.

The key is not to change who you are or what you are about but rather stay focused on your action plan and work towards your goal.

Understanding yourself is a crucial step before starting your job search. It's important to take time to reflect on personal strengths, weaknesses, and interests. This self-awareness can then be communicated effectively to recruiters, who are looking for candidates that not only fit the job description but also show potential for growth and alignment with the company's culture. One way to start this process is by taking personality tests, seeking feedback from friends and mentors, and reflecting on past experiences. This introspection can lead to a clearer career path and more meaningful conversations with potential employers. Remember, recruiters are not just looking for skills and experience; they're looking for a person who knows where they fit in the world of work.

In the journey of life, we find strength in our faith, believing that God will provide the guidance and support needed to navigate us through the complexities. This belief is a source of comfort and resilience for countless individuals, offering a sense of direction and purpose amidst life's challenges. It's a reminder

Activate Your Plan

that one is not alone in their struggles and that God can lead us through the darkest valleys to find peace and understanding. Faith in something greater gives us the courage to face each day with hope and determination. See it through your eyes of faith: "Then Jesus told his disciples a parable to show them that they should always pray and not give up" (Luke 18:1, NIV). Remember that God is faithful, and He is in charge.

An action plan will help you stay on top of your job search process. The goal of the action plan is to keep you moving and motivated. You may have to change your priorities or deadlines to keep your action plan moving.

Take action—no matter how small or difficult the first step may be. Avoid procrastination. Take baby steps if you are not feeling motivated. Change your mindset. Once you take one small action, it may inspire you to take more action. Or at least another action, and the next thing you know you have taken a few steps or a few hours toward the goal you set for yourself. Be flexible. Life is in a constant state of change. There is growth through transition. Go with the flow.

Review what you are doing in your job search and evaluate the process every now and then. If your approach is not working, change it. Get some ideas from your networking group or your networking contact buddy.

You will discover new things about yourself as you implement your job search plan. Taking things one step at a time is the only way to make progress. You have to take the outlined steps and prepare for the task ahead of you.

Keep focused on your goal, which is to be offered a job that you want. Never give up. What choice do you have? Yes, you can give up. But where will that leave you? We all experience setbacks. Look at searching for a job and posting resumes online as a challenge. It could get boring after a while, especially when you haven't made any progress towards your goal. You will reach your goal by not giving up, by perseverance and determination. Just keep going no matter what.

If you are feeling overwhelmed or down in the dumps, change it up. Do something different. Change what you are doing. Perhaps a short walk will be just the change of scenery you will need.

Stay committed to your job search no matter what it takes or no matter how long it takes. Do whatever is necessary to reach your ultimate goal of employment, no matter how difficult or monotonous it gets. And it will get monotonous after a few months. Check your expectations.

Keep yourself healthy mentally, physically, and spiritually to stay grounded. Preparedness for your daily action plan is key. Get yourself in the proper mindset at the beginning of every day. Activate your plan—don't put it off. Don't procrastinate.

Activate Your Plan

"This too shall pass." Eventually, you will be working again. Your current job status is temporary as with all things in life. Circumstances and situations are subject to change. In the meantime, yes, you will be faced with uncomfortable moments. There will be times when you are frustrated and say to yourself, Why do I have to do this? Why me? Work past those moments of self-doubt and impatience. Keep moving forward with your plan. Keep going. You are closer to your goal than you originally thought.

Know your resume inside and out. Know the work that you've done and the money you saved your previous employer. Know your work and reflect on the value you can offer to the job you are applying for.

Even if you feel an interview is not going well, complete the interview to the best of your ability.

Use effective words to excite and persuade the interviewer that you are ready and able to work. Listen to the interviewer. Listen, really listen. Be present. Don't let your mind wander. Pay attention. Listen to the questions being asked. Don't ramble on. Keep your responses short and to the point. Don't appear to be a know-it-all. Keep a good pace, a good balance.

Integrate examples of software programs on your resume you have learned. Provide examples of when you used those software programs during your interview.

The VIP Job Search

Write down a list of past accomplishments. Persistence is a top trait to carry through your job search. Make a daily list of all the positive steps you can take while searching for a job. Start with taking one step per day and increase additional steps until you are offered a job. Keep taking steps until you achieve the results you want. If a job lead a friend gave you did not work out, find another job lead. Keep it moving forward. Don't put all your energies into one job application or into one job lead.

Make a list of transferable skills, for example:

- Directed workflow
- Coaching
- Scheduling
- Finance
- Web-based software programs
- Budgets
- Negotiations
- Project management
- Communications
- Technology
- Interpersonal skills
- Created instructional materials
- Policies and procedures
- Conceptualized
- List awards on your resume

Activate Your Plan

What is your area of expertise? What do you do better than anyone else? Know your worth and salary expectations.

Don't expect your potential employer to "read between the lines." Tell your story in a cover letter with accomplishments listed clearly on your resume. An interview is an opportunity to "tell your story," to tell the prospective employer what you can do for them. Do your research prior to the interview, find out what employers are looking for, and use that information to your advantage.

How proficient are your skills? Employers want dependable, enthusiastic workers with a working knowledge of business and technology skills.

Make a list of your personal traits. Match your skills and abilities to the needs of the employer. Sift through the job description and match the companies' requirements to your abilities to determine what to include in your response. Include your own unique talents, skills, and abilities. Prioritize your assets that fit the position. Those are the ones that you would want to stand out on your resume.

Keep up with leading-edge research and development with webinars and online classes. By taking an active role in your learning you gain an edge and become more marketable. Focus on your successes. Reflect on accomplishments on your resume, not your work duties or tasks: verifiable percentages, amounts, and quantities. Every resume should be tailored to the position you are applying.

Being out of work, stuck in a dead-end job, or wanting to make a career change can devastate your self-esteem. Do not diminish your sense of self-worth by berating yourself. You are more than your occupation. You have talents, skills, and experience unique to you. Negative feelings keep you stuck. A positive attitude can give you a feeling of being in control with an expectation of better things to come. Take responsibility. Stay focused on the positive thought that things will work out. Be cheerful. *Smile!*

Take a risk. Even taking a small risk will do a lot to ease unfounded fears and eliminate negative self-talk. There will always be unanticipated problems, no matter how much planning you do. Increase your flexibility by breaking out of your normal routine and trying different things. Persistence makes a difference. Take a course. Update your skills. Work on developing relationships in your network. Schedule an appointment with your local unemployment office and make an appointment with a career advisor. Call someone in your networking group and schedule or arrange a brainstorming session. There is always something you could do. Your self-confidence will improve as you become successful at handling the unexpected.

Activate Your Plan

Listen to the questions being asked during the interview. Listen to the interviewer instead of preparing in your head over and over again what you want to say. We get anxious and want to tell our story. Stay calm and pray if you have to during this process. Most importantly, listen to what the interviewer is saying.

Pay attention and do not be distracted by formulating an answer in your mind to the question. Help the interviewer visualize your talents by providing a visual picture of what you can bring to your prospective employer.

The art of acing a job interview extends beyond your experience and qualifications listed on your resume. It's about presenting yourself as the complete package. As a child of God, dressing well and believing, acting, talking, and walking as if you are blessed can set the tone for the interview. Your confidence (including your put-together appearance) can signal to potential employers that you are ready and serious about the job opportunity. A tidy, neutral background during a Zoom interview minimizes distractions and keeps the focus on you. This attention to detail not only impresses interviewers but also boosts your self-confidence, reinforcing a positive self-image.

Embracing excellence is a lifestyle choice. It reflects a commitment to quality that employers value. The people you choose to surround yourself with can significantly influence your mindset. A network of positive and supportive individuals can inspire you to achieve greater heights, both professionally and personally. It's a virtuous cycle; success breeds success, and a positive environment fosters a mindset geared toward continuous improvement and fulfillment.

Prioritize tasks and allocate slots for each day on your calendar. If an unexpected networking opportunity arises, don't hesitate to rearrange your schedule to accommodate it. Networking events are invaluable; they not only provide potential job leads but also offer insights into industry trends and allow you to connect with peers. Remember, every interaction is a chance to make an impression, and every meeting is a step forward. So, push past any reluctance and embrace each opportunity with enthusiasm. The effort you put into networking and job searching today could very well shape your career tomorrow.

The philosophy of "one day at a time" is a powerful approach to life. It's a reminder that while we cannot control everything that happens to us, we can control our reactions and how we choose to live each day. By focusing on the present, setting daily goals, and maintaining flexibility, we build resilience and gradually progress toward our larger goals. Success is often the result of small, persistent steps forward. This not only helps in coping with life's unpredictability but also in appreciating the journey. Each day, as we grow closer to God, He leads us on our journey to success, building blocks not only to reach our goals but also to further God's kingdom.

Activate Your Plan

Second Thessalonians 1:6–8 (NIV) says, "God is just. He will pay trouble to those who trouble you and give relief to you who are troubled and to us as well." God's divine justice is, ultimately, the highest authority that oversees the moral balance of the world. This perspective encourages individuals to seek a personal relationship with the divine, to engage in introspection, and to find solace in the notion that there is a greater plan at work beyond what may be immediately apparent. It's a reminder that while life's challenges may seem insurmountable at times, many find comfort in faith and the belief in a just and attentive presence guiding the course of events.

__HR insider tip.__ Take one action step daily toward your job search goal. These steps will build upon each other, bringing you closer to your end goal, which is gainful employment.
In the journey toward securing employment, it is essential to adopt a strategic approach by taking consistent, actionable steps every day. This methodical progression involves identifying daily objectives that contribute to the larger goal of job acquisition. By breaking down the process into management tasks, such as refining your resume, networking with industry professionals, or learning new skills relevant to your desired field, you create a structured path forward. Each step builds momentum and confidence. It's the cumulative effect of these daily efforts that can lead to significant progress and, ultimate-

ly, the successful attainment of a fulfilling career. Consistency is key. Even the smallest actions can have a profound impact over time.

Chapter 6:

It's All About Your Mindset

"Do not conform to the pattern of this world, but be transformed by the renewing of your mind."

Romans 12:2 (NIV)

Attitude is a reflection of one's inner beliefs and perspectives, which can significantly influence the trajectory of one's life. A positive mindset often correlates with a life filled with opportunities and contentment, while a negative outlook can lead to a self-fulfilling prophecy of dissatisfaction and missed chances. It's not uncommon for individuals to experience a range of emotions, including anger or frustration, but the key lies in how these emotions are managed and transformed into constructive action.

People's perceptions of an individual can be greatly affected by the energy they exude. If someone frequently exhibits a cheerful and optimistic demeanor, they tend to attract others who appreciate and resonate with that positivity. Conversely, a consistently irritable or negative attitude may repel others, leading to isolation. It's important to note that everyone has the capacity for change, and altering one's thought patterns can have a profound impact on their life experiences.

The concept of "retraining" one's thoughts is rooted in cognitive behavioral principles, suggesting that by consciously choosing more positive and adaptive thoughts, individuals can reshape their experiences and reactions to life's challenges. This mental shift doesn't happen overnight; it requires dedication and practice. However, the rewards of such efforts result in improved relationships, better stress management, and a general increase in well-being.

Ultimately, the thoughts and attitudes one harbors are the driving forces behind your actions and decisions. By cultivating a mindset that embraces positivity, resilience, and adaptability,

It's All About Your Mindset

individuals can create a life that not only they enjoy but also inspires others around them. It's a journey of self-discovery and growth, where each thought is a step toward a more fulfilling and purposeful existence.

Change your thoughts about yourself. Level up your thoughts to a higher and different way of thinking. Think of the impossible. Think your life to the next level. What does that next level look like? What is your life's vision?

This applies to the task many job seekers avoid, which is the creation of a cover letter. Creating a cover letter template that you can use over and over again not only simplifies the job search process, it makes your resume stand out above the rest. Most people don't take the time to create a cover letter tailored to the job they are interested in applying for. In addition to using keywords, using a cover letter increases the chances that your resume will be viewed by the recruiter.

This is just one small step—one small example of thinking differently. Many people think it's too hard or takes too much time to write a cover letter for every job application. In addition, many people don't take the time to include "keywords" in their cover letter or resume. Change your mindset. While unemployed, I would ask myself this question: why not? I have the time. I'm unemployed. I've heard, time and time again, people complain and get upset over the work and time it takes to tailor a cover letter and resume with keywords for every job application. The response? That's a lot of work. That takes time. Yes, it does take work and it does take time. My question is, Aren't you worth it? Isn't it worth taking the extra time to make yourself stand out from the rest of the job applications received online? This is a vital step in the journey of the job search process, and most people do not take it. It's the small changes, small differences. Taking the time to write a cover letter and include keywords actually makes you stand out as a candidate. This is the difference-maker for an individual looking for a job. If you don't take the time and pay attention to the details, your resume will not stand out.

The job market can be incredibly competitive, and it's not uncommon for job seekers to send out a high volume of resumes in the hopes of securing employment. I have often met individuals who have submitted sixty to a hundred job applications in one month. This approach involves distributing resumes broadly rather than tailoring them to specific positions. The frustration for job seekers is the lack of response from employers acknowledging receipt of their job application. Instinctively, I knew there were two main reasons for a lack of employer response: (1) missing cover letter and (2) missing "keywords" throughout the cover letter and resume. Individuals seeking employment complain about what a tight job market it is out there today. Yes, that is true, so you need to think out of the box and do what it takes to obtain employment. There are no shortcuts to success in life.

It's All About Your Mindset

You must do what you don't feel like doing. People who are a success and stand out from the crowd, take steps that others may think about—but don't take action on. Yes, the job market is challenging. Taking the time to understand and learn aspects of the hiring process can help job seekers refine their approach and increase their visibility.

As a child of God, we are representatives of what it means to be Christians, which includes doing our best. If an individual decides not to take the steps necessary to obtain employment in a very competitive and global job market, this will result in missed opportunities. If you do not adapt, adjust, or change your actions, unemployment will stretch out for a longer period of time. Re-evaluate your action steps and determine if you need to make any changes in your approach.

Practical ways to foster positive thinking include focusing on your strengths, practicing gratitude, and engaging in self-compassion. Begin by identifying and leveraging your personal strengths, which can shift your perspective and increase self-confidence. Gratitude can be cultivated through daily practices such as maintaining a gratitude journal, which trains the brain to recognize and appreciate the positives in life. Self-compassion involves treating yourself with the same kindness and understanding that you would offer to a friend. Additionally, shifting attention away from negative thoughts, perhaps through physical activity or mindfulness, can prevent rumination and promote a positive mindset. Incorporating these strategies into daily routines can gradually transform thought patterns and contribute to a more optimistic and resilient outlook.

Gratitude is a powerful tool, especially during the challenging times of a job search. It can transform the way one perceives their situation, turning what seems like a series of obstacles into a path lined with opportunities for growth and appreciation. Documenting daily gratitude for things like access to clean water, reliable transportation, or the simple comfort of a home can shift focus from scarcity to abundance. This practice not only enhances well-being but also puts into perspective the relative wealth one possesses. If you have more than $40 in the bank, you hold more financial resources than a significant portion of the global population. This realization can foster a sense of responsibility and motivation to make the most of one's circumstances, using gratitude as a stepping stone to further personal and professional development. Gratitude, therefore, is not just an exercise in recognition but a foundation for resilience and a positive outlook on life's journey.

A positive attitude is indeed a powerful catalyst for innovation. It not only rekindles the imagination but also fosters an environment where new ideas can flourish. This mindset is contagious, inspiring others and creating a dynamic atmosphere where creativity is valued and exploration encouraged. Conversely, a negative attitude can be detrimental, stifling creativity and spreading discontent. It's essential for individuals and organizations alike to cultivate positivity as it can transform challenges into positive results.

Focusing your brain on the goals you have set for yourself actually changes the way you think. When you focus, it helps you change and turn away from those unhealthy patterns that do not serve you any longer.

Training our brains to think differently starts with prayer, reading Scripture, and making a decision. That decision is to change your life and change the results you are receiving, along with a decision to live more fully. When you focus on your goals, you become more motivated, happier, and more excited about your life.

Thinking more positively does not happen overnight, and it is a process just like anything else. It is a journey and takes time. If you change how you think about your job search, your feelings will change. If you remain upset about losing your job or not obtaining employment right after graduating from college, this won't help you. Change your perception of how you think about these things. Change your view on what is happening in your life right now. This will help adjust your feelings. In order to create a different life and experience more positive results, it begins with thinking differently. Ask yourself whether what you feel and think on the inside is being reflected in your public demeanor.

Try something new to increase your self-confidence and consider yourself a valuable and worthwhile person. Take action. Surround yourself with positive people. These actions have a profound effect on how you feel about yourself. How you feel about yourself is determined by how you talk to yourself most of the time. Why not change any negative self-talk into something more positive? As you develop more self-esteem, believe in yourself, and are more confident, you will start to experience more successful interviews. The Bible says you are an overcomer. With God's help, you can do this.

Are you close-minded and set in your ways? Or are you open-minded and free? Are you open to learning or listening to new ideas or concepts? Ask yourself, what does your next job look like? What's important to you? Is it a shorter commute? Is it working from home? Salary? A possible career change? Thinking about what is important to you and what you'd like out of life will help you identify and narrow down the jobs you should apply for.

Take the time to ensure that your job search goals are in alignment with who you are and what you are all about. There will never be a perfect match; however, if you get close to what you want in life, that's pretty good. There is no job that is perfect, as we are aware of what we can and cannot tolerate. Therefore,

It's All About Your Mindset

choose from your list of job requirements on your priority list and be willing to be flexible.

- ➢ *Your inner thoughts:* What do you say to yourself? What is the tone of your inner voice? Is it more like an inner critic? Where did that critical voice come from? Perhaps that inner critical voice has been with you for so long that you accept anything that it tells you. You never questioned where that inner critic came from or how it evolved. Have you ever considered challenging your inner critic? This is a conversation you might want to have with God.
- ➢ *What is your dream?* What would you like to do? What does your ideal or dream life look like? Practice thinking about it; daydream about it. Make room for it in your mind. What's most important to you?
- ➢ *What are you searching for?* Find a way to enjoy every single moment of your life, regardless of your current circumstances. Whether you are seeking a career change or gainful employment, we are all seeking health, peace, family, and making a difference in the world.
- ➢ *Prayer:* Make time to pray every day. It is important to incorporate prayer and thinking time in your life. Thinking time provides us with an opportunity to reflect. We tend to plan so many aspects of our lives...

we never ask ourselves the why behind our choices or actions. We may be afraid to think about it, so we continue to keep ourselves busy.

➢ *Opportunity to grow:* Times of trials are an opportunity to learn something new about yourself or about the situation that occurred. People actually get to know themselves better and experience what they are made of during difficult or challenging times. Scripture: Second Corinthians 12:9–11 (NIV) says, "My grace is sufficient for you, for my power is made perfect in weakness."

See, when we try to live life without God, we have strife, get stressed, get angry, and want to control the outcome. We want what we want—when we want it. You see, God does not make bad things happen to us—no, we are all very good at making that happen on our own. You see, God gave everyone free will; that is, He gave every human being the option to choose to have a relationship with Him or not.

There is nothing more soothing or calming in life than knowing that we don't need to go about life alone. Deuteronomy 31:6 (NIV) says, "Be strong and courageous. Do not be afraid or terrified because of them, for the Lord your God goes with you; he will never leave you nor forsake you." The problem is we try to do this thing called "life" on our own. God promised never to leave us nor forsake us. Life is hard enough for Christians who follow

It's All About Your Mindset

Christ and pray to God. However, we do have an understanding that God will always protect us and be with us.

> *Learn some new skills:* Take advantage of online classes through LinkedIn, your local library, community college, YouTube, or your local unemployment office. Learning new skills or keeping your skills current will make you more valuable to your prospective employer. Use any opportunity to learn something new, as this helps you maintain a positive attitude and improves your self-esteem.

> *Reduce stress:* Go for a walk, socialize with friends, read, or take a mini vacation. Embarking on a road trip to explore a long-desired destination within your home state can be a wonderfully enriching experience. It offers the opportunity to delve into the local culture, history, and natural beauty that might have been overlooked in the hustle of daily life. Such a journey will satisfy the curiosity and provide a refreshing break from the job search routine, allowing for personal growth and the creation of lasting memories. You will gain a new perspective and come back to your job search relaxed and ready for your next step in the process.

➤ *Be proactive:* Change the title of your "To-Do" list to a "Goal" list. Making this one simple change makes it sound more interesting and exciting. A "To-Do" list sounds like the chores you need to complete, things that are not that much fun, like laundry, grocery shopping, cleaning, etc. Goals—even the sound of the word is more appealing. Change how you think and feel about the things you need to do to obtain success. Say things to yourself such as, "This will only take a few minutes / twenty minutes / thirty minutes." Once I finish this task, then I can relax. Once I make these phone calls and send these emails, I can then take a walk. Take the afternoon off. Don't make it more complicated than it has to be.

➤ *Enrich your soul:* Try something new. Change your perspective. Change the way you've always done something in your life, even if it's driving to the gym, to the grocery store, or for a walk in your neighborhood. Drive down a different street. Go to a movie by yourself. See a comedy and stay away from the news. Making minor changes in your life will add up over time, and it will change your perspective. Driving down a different street to the grocery store or to the gym, you get to see new homes and different landscaping designs. Your mind starts to become more

It's All About Your Mindset

aware when you change things up. It's a small step toward moving out of your comfort zone, so you'll gain the courage and strength to try to move on and try something else. Next thing you know, you'll be applying for that job you know you deserve and are qualified for instead of settling and applying for "any job" because you want to work again. You deserve more. You deserve better. Be creative. Move away from the routine of what is familiar and get rid of the "this is the way I've always done it" attitude. Change your habits. Explore life. Dream and think about different options. It just may lead you to more innovative ways to think about and handle your job search.

> ➢ *Why do you want a job? Why do you want to work here?* There is a good chance you'll be asked these questions during the interview process. Be sure to have a well-thought-out response, and practice responding to your interview questions. You are competing with other candidates for this position, so have an answer prepared prior to the interview. Besides the obvious salary (money), what do you hope to gain from working?

Read or do something you enjoy, like work on a hobby. Perhaps you can try a new hobby. Meditate; practice time management. Clear out the clutter in your home office or workspace. Declutter and get organized while listening to your favorite music in the background. Dance while you are decluttering and reorganizing your home office. You'll feel better.

Keep busy doing things you love to do. Sure, you are working on your job search; however, it is healthy to take a break from the job search process. Otherwise, you could get burnt out and discouraged.

Take control of your mind, your thoughts, and your life. Become more disciplined. The journey of job searching is one that unfolds with each step taken, each resume sent, and each interview attended. It's a narrative of resilience, a testament to the human spirit's capacity to strive for progress and fulfillment. The process can be daunting, but it's also an opportunity for growth and self-discovery. It's about learning to navigate the complexities of the job market, understanding the value of one's skills and experiences, and finding the right fit where one can contribute and thrive.

Maintaining a positive mindset is crucial. The thoughts that occupy the mind can shape the trajectory of the job search. Positive self-talk can be a powerful tool, transforming doubts and fears into confidence and action. It's about affirming one's worth and capabilities, recognizing that each individual brings a unique set of skills and experiences to the table. God gave us all unique talents and abilities. Our prayer life and positive internal dialogue can open doors to opportunities that align with one's career aspirations and values.

Taking control of one's thoughts is akin to steering a ship through turbulent waters. It requires discipline, focus, and a clear vision of the destination. It's about setting realistic goals, breaking them down into manageable tasks, and celebrating each small victory along the way. This disciplined approach can help in maintaining momentum, even when faced with setbacks or rejections.

Remember, the job search is not just about finding a position—it's about finding a path that aligns with one's passions and life story. It's a chapter in a larger narrative, one that speaks to the individual's journey towards personal and professional fulfillment. So, take those small steps, keep the inner voice positive, and trust in the process. The right opportunity will come, and when it does, it will be a fitting addition to the story of a life well-lived, marked by faith, perseverance, and success.

Act on the truth that God wants us to ask Him for help with all our needs. Walk in the confidence that God always answers us with His help (see Psalm 34). Prayer is believing in miracles—*not coincidence*! Don't be "blind" to God's workings in your life. Believe in *"providence,"* not in *"coincidence!"*

What is your story? What kind of story are you telling with your life. Is it a life full of faith, perseverance, and patience? The job search journey can feel overwhelming; this is a narrative shared by many. It's a tale of resilience, patience, and personal and spiritual growth. The process, while daunting, is not just about the destination but also about the transformation that occurs along the way. Pray over each application sent, each interview attended, and each networking opportunity, which will contribute to God's miracle-working power in "your" story.

This story is not solely about faith and success; it's also about the setbacks and the lessons learned from them. It's about the days filled with hope and the nights filled with doubt and the courage to continue despite them. It's about the small victories in improving a resume, the clarity gained from a career counseling session, or the insights from feedback on an interview.

The narrative of a job search is complex, filled with characters such as potential employers, mentors, peers, and family members who provide support and advice. It's a story that unfolds in chapters, each job application representing a new possibility, a new "what if."

In this story, the protagonist—you—grows. With each step, you become more adept at articulating your value, more resilient in the face of rejection, and more knowledgeable about the industry you aspire to join. The plot thickens with each new lead, each informational interview, and each revised cover letter, building toward the climax of landing the job.

And while the desire to skip to the final page is understandable, it's the preceding pages that make the ending worthwhile.

It's All About Your Mindset

They are filled with moments of self-discovery, skill enhancement, and, sometimes, unexpected opportunities.

So, while the job search process will take time, and it may seem overwhelming, remember that this is your story. It's one where taking small steps is not just advisable; it's necessary. It's a story where each chapter builds upon the last and where the protagonist's journey is just as important as the end goal. In the grand narrative of your career, this is but one of many stories you will tell, and like all good stories, the challenges faced are what make the triumphs so rewarding.

Remember, every job seeker has their own unique story, and yours is just beginning. It's a story of growth, learning, and eventual success as long as you keep turning the pages, one small step at a time.

Life's inherent unfairness often leads to feelings of anger and frustration, particularly when faced with challenging circumstances that seem undeserved. It's a natural human reaction to question why these events occur, especially when one strives to live a good and just life. The emotional journey through anger is a valid and sometimes necessary part of processing these experiences. However, it's crucial to recognize the potential for such emotions to evolve into a more debilitating state, such as depression, if they are allowed to fester unaddressed.

The advice to not become one's own worst enemy is sage; it's essential to find constructive ways to deal with life's adversities. Turning to faith, Scripture, or personal beliefs can provide solace and guidance during tumultuous times. It's a reminder that while it's acceptable to feel anger and to grieve losses—such as the loss of a job—it's also important to reflect on one's role in the events that unfold in life. Sometimes, the realization that a change was needed comes only in hindsight, highlighting the importance of being proactive in making decisions about one's future.

Taking ownership of one's path can be empowering. It involves recognizing when situations are not beneficial and having the courage to take steps toward change. This can mean leaving a job that no longer serves one's growth, or it could involve seeking new opportunities that align more closely with one's values and aspirations. It's about not leaving one's future solely in the hands of others but rather taking an active role in shaping it.

Ultimately, the journey through anger and frustration toward acceptance and proactive change is deeply personal and can be complex. It requires patience, self-compassion, and the willingness to seek and accept support when needed. By focusing on personal growth and resilience, one can navigate life's unfair moments with grace and emerge with a stronger sense of self and purpose.

Keep a positive mindset. On those difficult days of your job search when you don't want to follow this process any longer, keep things in perspective. Remember that God is in control and that He hears your prayers. Trust in His Word.

It's All About Your Mindset

Your unemployment status is temporary. Be patient, as your desire to get a better job and quickly get out of the situation you are in will only frustrate you. God may be developing more patience within you. Be diligent, and stay focused and full of prayer. Be grateful for your every day. Trust that things are unfolding as they are meant to. There is a Scripture to keep you grounded; please read Psalm 39:7 (TLB): "My only hope is in you."

***HR insider tip.** Reading biographies about individuals who have overcome significant challenges can be incredibly inspiring. These narratives often highlight the resilience of the human spirit and provide valuable lessons on perseverance, adaptability, and the power of a positive outlook. Starting each day with a positive mindset can set the tone for the hours ahead, influencing our interactions, productivity, and overall well-being. Positive thinking isn't just about ignoring life's stressors but rather about approaching them with the right attitude—believing in our ability to cope and find solutions. This approach can indeed be a source of strength and comfort, offering moments of peace amidst chaos and helping to maintain a balanced perspective on life's ups and downs.*

Avoiding negative influences is equally important, as they can hinder one's progress and mental health. Consulting with a professional counselor can be a valuable step, and it's beneficial to know that many health insurance plans provide coverage for mental health services.

Chapter 7:

Community of Support

"I hear counsel, receive instruction, and accept correction that I may be wise in the time to come."

Proverbs 19:20 (paraphrased)

Building a supportive community during challenging times is a vital endeavor that can provide comfort, resilience, and a sense of belonging. To foster such a community, it's essential to start by identifying common interests or goals that can unite people. Creating a space—whether physical or virtual—where individuals feel safe to share and be themselves is crucial. Engaging in active listening and open communication helps to build trust and understanding among members. It's also beneficial to encourage the sharing of resources and skills, as mutual aid can strengthen community bonds.

Organizing regular meetings or events can maintain a sense of continuity and presence. Additionally, recognizing and celebrating the diversity within the community can lead to a richer, more inclusive environment. Remember, the process of building a community is ongoing and requires patience, empathy, and a willingness to adapt to the needs of its members.

There are some individuals who feel intimidated by the use of social media. This may hamper their job search process as it is difficult for today's recruiters to find qualified applicants. A LinkedIn account gives HR recruiters an opportunity to view your background and, perhaps, make a match with a job opening they have at their company. The act of sharing one's challenges and finding unexpected assistance from acquaintances rather than long-term friends can be surprising, yet it highlights the unpredictable nature of human connections. Such experiences can prompt a rethinking of what constitutes a friend and lead to a reshuffling of one's social network, prioritizing those who offer positivity and genuine support. It's a reminder that, sometimes,

Community of Support

support comes from the least expected places, and the willingness to extend a helping hand can forge new, meaningful friendships.

Ultimately, navigating the complexities of joblessness and job hunting is not just about securing employment; it's also about understanding the dynamics of human relationships and the importance of nurturing a supportive community. It's about learning to discern who in one's life adds value and positivity and making the conscious choice to surround oneself with those individuals. This process of social selection is a natural response to the desire for a harmonious and encouraging environment, especially during challenging times. It's a testament to the human capacity for adaptation and the pursuit of happiness, even in the face of adversity. The resilience shown in such situations is a powerful affirmation of one's ability to overcome obstacles and emerge stronger, with a clearer sense of self and a redefined circle of trust.

Networking makes our job search easier when qualified, competent people are able to impart valuable contact information, job leads, technological expertise, and industry information. Strategize on how to ace your next interview. Ask for referrals. Build quality relationships with people. If you work the room and pass out dozens of business cards, this type of behavior could suggest insincerity.

Building a network is also a strategic move, as it can provide support, open doors to new opportunities, and offer diverse perspectives that can enhance one's understanding and skills.

Tips for successful networking include the following:

- Raise your visibility. Do not limit networking to times when you need something.
- Be friendly and sincere, and remember people's names.
- Step outside your comfort zone and meet new people.
- Generally, care about people.
- Respect others.
- Stay in touch.
- Express an interest in others.
- Share ideas.
- Be positive and confident.
- Join in discussions.
- Wear a name tag at events.
- Do not pester your contacts.
- Continually add to your network.
- Connect with your contacts on a regular basis.

It's important to recognize the value you bring to your relationships and to look for positive and encouraging individuals. Re-evaluating your circle of influence is not just about distancing yourself from negativity but also about acknowledging

Community of Support

your worth and the quality of life you deserve. Networking with like-minded individuals can open doors to opportunities and foster a community of mutual support, which is beneficial in all phases of life, whether you're seeking employment or thriving in your career. Remember, the quality of your connections often reflects the quality of your experiences.

Build long-term relationships. Improve your job search techniques. Join a professional association to meet professionals in your industry. Put yourself out there to build a beneficial network. Have someone to call for support when you are feeling down about your job search. Networking is indeed a dynamic and unpredictable process where one can meet a diverse group of individuals, ranging from those gainfully employed to those seeking opportunities. Guest speakers at networking events can provide valuable insights and connections that may lead to job prospects. Follow up with new contacts. Fostering professional relationships on LinkedIn can expand one's network and visibility. Prayer, or any form of reflection and planning, can serve as a means to organize one's life and priorities, which is essential for personal organization and development.

Build a network of positive people who will benefit and sustain you. Be prepared to tell your story. Who are you? Why do you do what you do? How did you get into the field? What makes your story different than the other candidates? What can you offer that others don't?

- Look at the job description.
- Write in your notebook how your background fits into what is required in the job description.
- Always submit your resume with a cover letter. (It makes you stand out. Is it time-consuming? Yes; however, it is worth it.) A cover letter enhances your resume and provides an opportunity for you to *tell your story*.

There is a lack of understanding and empathy from people who are currently employed toward those who have experienced a job loss. In the past, people worked at the same job for many, many years, and for a number of years, this has no longer been the case. In today's job marketplace, there is an enormous transition in many industries, which makes anyone's job temporary.

If it's been a while since you've been in a job interview, you will be in for a shock as the process is so different than years ago. You will learn rather quickly that this is not the same job search process you might have experienced previously in your career. Today, the job search process is very unpredictable and has been for the last ten to twelve years.

God is the same yesterday, today, and tomorrow. He is the constant in your life. He will never change. Ask Him for help and to guide you through the difficult job application and interview process.

Community of Support

People are human, and they will disappoint you. Recruiters will tell you they will give you a call by the end of the week, and you will never hear from them. Hiring managers will tell you that you are perfect for the job, and you will find that they never get in touch with you again.

After six months of being unemployed, I interviewed for a position on a Wednesday, which was close to the end of my unemployment benefits. I had been at the company for a few hours when the last person I interviewed with said to me, "You are perfect for this job based on your experience. Could you start on Monday?"

I said, "Absolutely, yes."

I was told I would receive a phone call by Friday with instructions as to how to prepare for work when I would show up on Monday. Unfortunately, that was thirteen years ago and I never received a phone call from the employer.

My point in telling this interview experience is when you go on an interview, do your best. Send the follow-up thank you emails. Be sure to thank the individuals in person for their time. Let the interviewer know you are interested in the position. Provide them with your contact information. And then let it go. Move on to the next interview. Don't hound these people. Don't put all your eggs in one basket. In other words, people say things and make promises that are not true. I do believe that many times people who are part of the interview process are not trained and don't know how to respond or what to do. Don't take this personally, as it has nothing to do with you. It's not your fault, and you could not have done anything else to change the situation.

The important part is what you do—what action you take after a situation like this. My recommendation is to keep on moving with the job search process. Don't stop applying for jobs, no matter what people tell you during an interview. Until you are sitting in that cubicle, behind the desk and start working, keep moving forward with the interview process.

I recall a colleague of mine who was out of work for a very long time. She went on an interview and was told she was perfect for the job and that they would be reaching out to her soon with a job offer. She was ecstatic about the position and more than happy to put her job search behind her. I recommended, ever so gingerly (so as not to dash her dreams), that it would be a good idea for her to keep up with her job search efforts. She did not take my HR experience into consideration and waited to hear from the employer. Three months after the interview, she received a letter in the mail informing her that the "position was filled" with another hire.

No matter how great the interview and no matter what you were told, until you receive that offer letter and are sitting in the seat of your new job, keep up with your job search.

Community of Support

This is where God becomes more important in our lives as we rely on Him and not on what people say. God is always truthful to His Word. God says in the Bible, in Numbers 23:19, "God is not a man, that he should lie."

For example, when a recruiter or hiring manager informs you that you are a perfect fit for the job, be gracious and complete all the interview protocols. However, do not, under any circumstance, stop looking for work. Now, we are all frustrated with the online application system, people not getting back to us, people not being responsive, and not following up. Don't take it personally. Especially in HR, the department may be short-staffed. People may be out on vacation or out sick. You just don't know. Don't always make it about you. In other words, don't blame yourself for things that are out of your control.

By focusing on your path and doing the best you can, keep your head straight and your eyes focused on God, as He is a God of restoration. I lay all my cares at God's feet, no matter how great or small.

Remember, the job search is not just about finding a position—it's about finding a path that aligns with one's passions and life story. It's a chapter in a larger narrative, one that speaks to the individual's journey toward personal, professional, and spiritual fulfillment. So, take those small steps, keep the inner voice positive, and trust in the process. The right opportunity will come, and when it does, it will be a fitting addition to the story of a life well-lived, marked by faith, perseverance, and success.

HR insider tip. *In the professional realm, having a "buddy" within a job networking group can be an excellent strategy for mutual support and idea sharing. This partnership allows for a collaborative approach to problem-solving and can be particularly beneficial during challenging times. A supportive network understands the ups and downs of the job search process and can offer encouragement and advice when needed. Overall, these practices can foster a sense of community, resilience, and optimism, which are essential for personal and professional growth.*

Creating a supportive environment is essential for personal growth and well-being. It involves building relationships with individuals who provide encouragement and understanding. Seeking support from a community, such as a church group, can offer a sense of belonging and additional resources for coping with life's trials and tribulations. This proactive approach to cultivating a positive support system is a commendable strategy for enhancing one's quality of life.

Chapter 8:

Interviews and the Internet

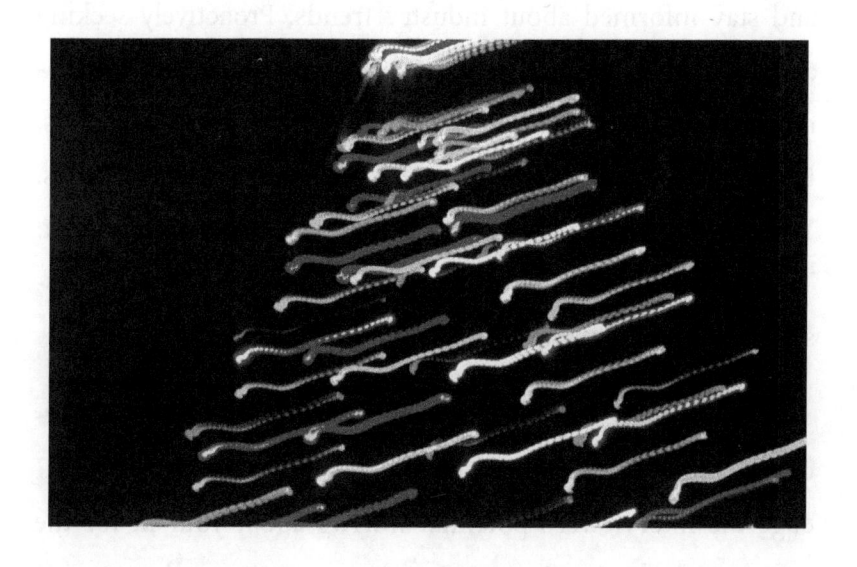

"When I go someplace and the people don't receive and accept me, I don't let it get me down. I just shake it off and go about my business."

Luke 10:10–11 (paraphrased)

When embarking on a job search, it's crucial to reflect on your career goals and personal needs. Consider whether you're seeking the same type of role as before or you're aiming for a career shift. Financial needs often dictate urgency, but aligning a job with long-term career aspirations is equally important. Balancing work hours with personal life, updating skills through courses, and networking can significantly enhance job prospects. Embrace mistakes made in interviews as learning experiences and stay informed about industry trends. Proactively seeking and even creating job opportunities can set you apart. Temporary positions can offer flexibility and exposure to different roles. Remember, self-care, including rest, is vital during this process. Volunteering can expand your network and provide fulfillment. Throughout this journey, maintaining a positive outlook is essential, as perseverance often leads to success.

When facing an interview where you're perceived as overqualified, it's crucial to address the concern directly. Acknowledge the interviewer's potential worries about your fit for the role, but emphasize the unique value you bring and your genuine interest in the position. It's beneficial to express a strong commitment to the company and articulate how your extensive experience will contribute positively.

Confidence is key, yet it should be balanced with humility to avoid appearing arrogant. Discussing long-term career goals that align with the company's vision can also reassure the interviewer of your intentions to stay and grow within the organization.

Moreover, conveying passion for the work and the company culture can help shift the focus from being overqualified to being an asset that can drive the company forward. Lastly, being open to discussions about compensation shows flexibility and a focus on the role's intrinsic rewards rather than just the financial aspect.

Understanding oneself is crucial when entering the job market, as it equips an individual with the necessary self-awareness to effectively communicate their strengths and values to potential employers. Self-knowledge serves as the foundation for personal branding, allowing one to craft a narrative that highlights unique skills, experiences, and qualities that align with the needs of the organization. It enables a person to answer questions with confidence and authenticity, demonstrating not only a fit for the role but also a genuine passion and understanding of how they can contribute to the company's goals.

Moreover, self-awareness facilitates the identification of areas for improvement, which can be addressed through continuous learning and development, further enhancing one's appeal to employers. It also aids in the articulation of career aspirations and how these intersect with the opportunities provided by the prospective employer, creating a compelling case for one's candidacy.

In essence, the process of self-discovery is an investment in one's professional future. It allows for a more targeted job search, where one can seek out positions and companies that resonate with their values and career objectives. This strategic approach not only increases the likelihood of job satisfaction but also positions an individual as a valuable asset to employers, who are often seeking candidates with a clear sense of direction and purpose.

Therefore, taking the time to introspect and understand one's professional identity is not just about selling oneself in an interview; it's about forging a career path that is both fulfilling and aligned with one's personal and professional goals. It's about being able to communicate not just what one can do but who one is and how that identity adds value to an organization. In the competitive landscape of job hunting, self-knowledge is the differentiator that can make one stand out in a sea of applicants. It's the key to not just landing a job but building a meaningful career.

Understanding what is important to oneself is crucial when interviewing for a job. It's not just about showcasing your skills and experience; it's also about assessing whether the company's culture, values, and career opportunities align with your personal and professional goals. Knowing your priorities, such as work-life balance, professional development, or the impact of your work, can guide you in asking insightful questions and evaluating job offers. This self-awareness ensures that the job you accept is more than just a paycheck but a step toward fulfilling your career aspirations and personal contentment.

Interviews and the Internet

Preparing for an interview can be a daunting task, but having a set of sample questions can be a great way to start. Common interview questions often revolve around your previous experience, such as "Tell me about yourself," "Walk me through your resume," or "What is your greatest professional achievement?" Employers may also be interested in your problem-solving skills with questions like: "Tell me about a challenge or conflict you've faced at work and how you dealt with it." It's not just about past experiences; future-oriented questions are also popular, such as "Where do you see yourself in five years?" or "What are your career aspirations?" To prepare, consider your answers to these questions, focusing on concrete examples that showcase your skills and adaptability. Remember, the goal is to demonstrate that you are the best fit for the role and the company culture. You may find a comprehensive list of common interview questions and tips on how to answer them on the internet, such as Yahoo, Google, Indeed, or LinkedIn.

Preparing for an interview involves a multifaceted approach, ensuring you're ready to discuss various aspects of the job and how they align with your personal and professional goals. It's crucial to research the salary range for the position you're applying for, which can be found on websites like Glassdoor or by reaching out to professionals in the field via LinkedIn. Understanding the typical commute and hours expected for the role is also important as it impacts your daily life and work-life balance.

Reflect on what you consider an acceptable commute and work hours, and be prepared to discuss these preferences during the interview. Additionally, inquire about the possibility of travel requirements, as this can significantly affect your routine and lifestyle. By addressing these elements, you demonstrate to potential employers that you are thorough in your preparation and considerate of how the job fits into your broader career aspirations. Remember, an interview is not just about them evaluating you; it's also an opportunity for you to assess whether the job aligns with what you're looking for in your next career move.

Preparing for a job interview is akin to strategizing for a critical presentation. It involves a deep understanding of the role you're applying for, the company's culture, and how your skills and experiences align with the company's needs. Crafting tailored responses to potential interview questions not only demonstrates your qualifications but also your proactive approach and dedication to excellence. This level of preparation signals to the interviewer that you possess the foresight and commitment necessary to excel in the role. Moreover, it showcases your ability to anticipate challenges and prepare solutions in advance, which are valuable traits in any job. Ultimately, the confidence and readiness you exhibit in an interview can be a strong indicator of your future performance and adaptability in the workplace.

When evaluating a company's potential for growth, it is essential to review its latest press releases and financial statements. These documents can provide insights into the company's year-over-year growth and its future expansion plans. For instance, lululemon has announced a five-year growth plan aiming to double revenue by 2026, focusing on product innovation, guest experience, and market expansion. Similarly, Starbucks has introduced a three-year financial roadmap with targeted investments expected to drive long-term growth and expand operating margin. Johnson & Johnson has also shared its long-term financial targets, expecting operational sales growth despite challenges. These examples illustrate how companies articulate their growth trajectories and strategic plans. Aligning a company's mission statement and plans with your personal plans and goals is crucial when considering a long-term investment or career opportunity. It ensures that the company's direction complements your objectives, potentially leading to a mutually beneficial relationship. Assessing these factors thoroughly will provide a clearer picture of the company's stability and prospects for growth.

Interviews can be a high-pressure situation, but with the right preparation, they offer a valuable opportunity to showcase your skills and fit for the role. Crafting concise, targeted interview questions can help you anticipate and articulate your responses effectively. Practicing in front of a mirror is an excellent way to observe your body language and ensure your answers are delivered with confidence and clarity. Remember, brevity is key; a succinct response that directly addresses the question is far more impactful than a lengthy monologue. Embrace moments of silence as they can give both you and the interviewer time to reflect and prepare for the next question. While nerves are natural, maintaining composure and a calm demeanor will convey confidence and professionalism. It's important to manage your stress and not let it show because the way you handle pressure is often as important as the answers you provide.

In an interview, showcasing the balance between soft skills and technical skills is crucial. Soft skills, such as communication, teamwork, and problem-solving, are often gauged through behavioral questions. These questions aim to reveal how you've applied these skills in real-world situations. For instance, an interviewer might ask about a time you faced a conflict on a team and how you resolved it. On the technical side, you might be asked to demonstrate your expertise through problem-solving exercises or discussing past projects. Prioritizing work often involves understanding the urgency and importance of tasks, which can be illustrated by explaining your method for handling deadlines and deliverables. When it comes to managing multiple projects, it's about showing your organizational skills and ability to multitask without compromising quality. An effective approach is to discuss how you allocate time, use project management tools, or delegate tasks to ensure all projects progress smoothly.

Understanding one's qualifications and aligning them with

the company's needs is a strategic approach to job interviews. Preparation is indeed crucial; it involves not only rehearsing potential questions but also refining how one communicates their unique strengths. This process ensures that responses are coherent, concise, and effectively showcase individual competencies. Such thorough preparation signals to potential employers a dedication to quality and an earnest pursuit of personal and professional growth. It's a testament to an individual's drive for success and their understanding of the value they bring to a prospective role.

The analogy of being the CEO of "You, Inc." is a powerful mindset when approaching job interviews. It emphasizes the importance of personal branding and the presentation of one's skills and experiences as valuable assets to potential employers. Just as a CEO must understand every aspect of their business, a job seeker should have a comprehensive understanding of their own qualifications and how they align with the needs of the company. Preparation is key, and practicing interview questions allows for the refinement of communication skills, ensuring that responses are not only well-structured but also tailored to highlight one's unique value proposition. This level of preparation demonstrates to employers a commitment to excellence and a proactive approach to professional development.

In the digital age, effective communication extends beyond

just the words we speak. During virtual meetings, such as those on Zoom or Teams, non-verbal cues are just as important. Your tone of voice can convey confidence or uncertainty, while your behavior and engagement level can demonstrate your interest or lack thereof. Facial expressions are particularly telling; a smile can be a powerful tool to create a positive atmosphere. It's essential to be mindful of these aspects to ensure that the message you intend to send is the one that is received.

Ensuring a professional background during a Zoom interview is crucial as it sets the stage for a focused and serious discussion. A cluttered or distracting background can divert attention away from the conversation, potentially undermining the professional image one aims to project. It's advisable to choose a neutral, tidy space with good lighting. If a suitable space isn't available, using a simple virtual background can be a good alternative. Additionally, checking all technical aspects, such as camera angle, sound quality, and internet connection, can help prevent any disruptions during the interview. Remember, the goal is to create an environment that allows both the interviewee and interviewer to concentrate on the dialogue without any unnecessary distractions.

First impressions are crucial in conveying the gravity of a situation. They set the tone for all subsequent interactions and can significantly influence someone's perception and response.

Interviews and the Internet

In order to make a serious and impactful first impression, it's important to communicate with clarity and confidence. Presenting well-organized thoughts, displaying a professional demeanor, and showing genuine concern or understanding of the matter at hand can help establish the necessary gravitas. It's also beneficial to provide clear evidence or reasoning to support your perspective, ensuring that the seriousness is not just felt but also understood logically. Remember, the goal is not just to impress but to engage the person deeply with the seriousness of the issue.

Preparing for an interview is a crucial step toward achieving professional success. It involves researching the company, understanding the role, and being able to articulate your experiences and how they align with the job requirements. Being prepared also means anticipating potential questions and practicing your responses to convey confidence and clarity. Professionalism is demonstrated through punctuality, appropriate attire, and respectful communication. Remember, a genuine smile can set a positive tone for the interaction, making you appear approachable and engaged. It's the subtle balance of preparation, professionalism, and personality that often makes a memorable impression.

When preparing for a behavioral interview, it's essential to reflect on past experiences that showcase your skills and adaptability. For example, when asked about accomplishments, you might discuss a project where you led a team to exceed its goals under a tight deadline, highlighting your leadership and time management skills. Overcoming challenges can be illustrated by a time you resolved a conflict within a team, emphasizing your communication and problem-solving abilities. Learning from experiences is crucial; perhaps you learned the importance of delegation and trust in team dynamics. To demonstrate continuous improvement, discuss your proactive approach to learning, such as regularly attending workshops or pursuing certifications relevant to your field. If asked about recent educational endeavors, mention the latest course you completed, which could be related to a new technology or methodology in your industry. Throughout the interview, maintain an enthusiastic demeanor, as positivity can be infectious and leave a lasting impression on the interviewer. Optimism not only reflects confidence but also shows resilience, a trait highly valued in any professional setting. Remember, each story you tell is an opportunity to present yourself as the solution to the employer's needs.

If you've experienced downsizing, it's understandable to feel disappointed; however, it's beneficial to focus on the future and the opportunities ahead. Expressing a constructive perspective on past experiences can demonstrate resilience and adaptability—qualities that are highly valued by HR professionals. They are not just assessing your skills for the job but also your potential to contribute positively to the team's dynamics and company culture.

Interviews and the Internet

Remember, every interview is a fresh start and a chance to make a strong impression that aligns with your career aspirations.

The job search process can indeed be, at times, disheartening. It's true that the effort put into tailoring resumes and cover letters for each application can be substantial, but this personalized approach often yields better results. By incorporating keywords from the job description, you align your qualifications with the employer's needs, making it more likely that your application will stand out. It's a strategic move in a competitive job market. Customizing applications shows potential employers that you are not only interested in the role but also diligent and attentive to detail. While it may be time-consuming, the quality of your applications can significantly influence the quantity and quality of responses you receive. Remember, every job application is an opportunity to present yourself as the best candidate for the position, and the extra work can be the deciding factor in landing the job you desire.

LinkedIn. Marketing oneself on the internet is a multifaceted endeavor that extends beyond social media platforms like Facebook or Instagram. LinkedIn, in particular, stands out as a critical tool for job seekers and professionals aiming to establish their presence in the job market. It's not just a platform for networking; it's a dynamic space where one can showcase their skills, experiences, and professional achievements. A well-crafted LinkedIn profile serves as a virtual resume and can significantly enhance visibility to recruiters and potential employers. In fact, many recruiters consider a LinkedIn profile a prerequisite before engaging with a candidate. It's a medium where professional identities are vetted and opportunities are explored. For those hesitant about joining LinkedIn, it's worth considering the platform's role in today's digital job market. It's a place where one can connect with industry leaders, participate in professional groups, and even access a wealth of job listings tailored to their skills and experience. In essence, a LinkedIn profile is more than just an online presence; it's a strategic tool for personal branding and career development.

Preparing for an in-person interview is indeed a significant milestone. Researching the company thoroughly can set you apart as a candidate. Start by exploring their website to understand their products, services, and company culture. Familiarize yourself with their latest projects and any expansion plans they might have, as this can be a great talking point. Additionally, it's beneficial to stay informed about the company's recent developments by checking news articles or press releases. This knowledge not only helps in making a good impression but also in asking insightful questions during the interview.

Staying proactive and maintaining momentum in your job search can lead to unexpected opportunities. It's important to keep moving forward, leveraging all available resources and

Interviews and the Internet

maintaining a positive outlook.

Perseverance in the job search is crucial, and your experience is a testament to the importance of resilience. The journey through unemployment is often challenging and filled with uncertainty, but maintaining a proactive approach is key. It's essential to utilize all available resources, such as networking, job fairs, and online job boards, and to consider various employment opportunities, even those outside one's usual field. Additionally, seeking support from career counselors, mentors, or support groups can provide guidance and encouragement. Financial planning and exploring temporary or part-time work can also be vital in managing expenses during this period. Your determination and persistence are admirable, and they serve as a powerful reminder that giving up is not an option when facing adversity.

The journey of job searching can indeed be a challenging and sometimes lengthy process. It's important to remember that each experience, whether it's attending networking events or refining your resume, is a step toward your goal. Keeping faith and persistence is key.

It's also beneficial to take a strategic approach: Start by listing your skills and achievements. Reflect on how these can be applied in various industries and roles. Don't hesitate to reach out to mentors or professionals in your desired field for advice and insights. Remember, every skill you've acquired is valuable and can open doors to opportunities you may not have considered. Stay positive and proactive, and soon, you'll find a role that's not just a job but a stepping stone to a fulfilling career. In the professional landscape, transferable skills are invaluable as they enable individuals to adapt to various job roles and industries. For instance, strong communication skills are essential in nearly every field, from customer service to management, allowing for effective exchange of ideas and fostering teamwork. Analytical skills, such as problem-solving and critical thinking, are also highly transferable, providing the ability to assess situations and make informed decisions, which is crucial in roles ranging from finance to healthcare. Additionally, technological proficiency, particularly in computer software and digital tools, has become a universal requirement, opening opportunities in numerous sectors. Leadership and project management skills can lead to roles in team coordination, project oversight, and strategic planning. By recognizing and honing these transferable skills, one can significantly broaden their job search and increase their adaptability in the ever-evolving job market.

Approaching a job interview with the right mindset is indeed a delicate art. It involves presenting oneself in a light that is both assured and receptive. Confidence is key, but it must be tempered with the grace of humility to avoid the pitfalls of appearing overconfident. Honesty, supported by tangible examples of past successes, speaks volumes about an individual's competence and potential contribution to a new role. It's about weaving a narrative that aligns with the company's values and culture, demonstrating not only what you have achieved but also how you can drive future success within the team. Ultimately, it's the blend of self-awareness, genuine enthusiasm for the role, and a clear understanding of how your skills map to the job that will resonate with potential employers.

Behavioral interviews are a critical component of the hiring process, as they offer employers a glimpse into how potential employees might fit within the company's culture and work environment. These interviews focus on past behavior as an indicator of future performance, emphasizing the importance of personal experiences and problem-solving skills. Networking plays a pivotal role in understanding the nuances of a company's social dynamics, providing insights that go beyond the surface level. It's essential to approach such information with discernment, recognizing that individual experiences may not represent the whole story. Ultimately, making informed decisions based on a combination of personal values, diverse perspectives, and thoughtful consideration can lead to fulfilling career paths that align with one's principles and aspirations.

Hang on to that positive attitude. Improving soft skills is a crucial aspect of personal and professional development, especially when one is seeking employment. A positive attitude is often the first step in this improvement process. It's important to manage emotions effectively; feelings of frustration or anger due to unemployment can inadvertently be conveyed during interviews, potentially affecting one's chances. Engaging with a variety of learning materials, such as books, podcasts, and educational videos, can introduce new perspectives and ideas. Applying these concepts in daily life can lead to growth and confidence outside one's comfort zone.

Maintaining a positive outlook during periods of unemployment can be challenging, yet it is essential for both mental well-being and job-seeking success. Embracing this time as an opportunity for growth and reflection can lead to personal development and a better understanding of one's career goals. It's important to stay proactive, using this period to enhance skills, network, and explore new career paths. Remember, every experience is a step forward, and with perseverance and optimism, the path to new employment will unfold.

In the journey of job searching, embracing challenges with a proactive mindset is crucial. Mastering technology is a vital skill that can significantly enhance employability in today's digital-centric job market. It's important to showcase one's strengths and past successes when applying for new roles, as this can illustrate to potential employers the unique value one can bring to their team. Engaging in daily productive activities, even those unrelated to job hunting, can help maintain a positive outlook and forward momentum. This comprehensive approach to self-improvement not only polishes soft skills but also shapes a well-rounded persona that is appealing to employers. Watching inspirational videos on platforms like YouTube can offer motivation and remind individuals that their current unemployment is temporary and a new working chapter is on the horizon.

In the nuanced dance of job interviews, effectively presenting oneself is indeed akin to an art form, requiring a deft touch and keen awareness of the interviewer's expectations. It's essential to strike a delicate balance between showcasing your experience and aligning it with the needs of the job at hand. Succinctness is key; brief yet impactful responses that draw direct lines between your skills and the job requirements can make a memorable impression. When prompted to share about yourself, it's not the length of your career narrative that counts but the relevance and clarity with which you connect your past achievements to potential future contributions. This strategic approach to interviewing, much like a well-executed improvisational performance, demands presence, adaptability, and a deep understanding of the role you're aiming to fill.

The concept of mindset, as proposed by psychologist Carol Dweck, has profound implications for personal development and learning. A fixed mindset, where individuals believe their abilities are static, can lead to a reluctance to face challenges or persist in the face of setbacks. This mindset can create a self-imposed barrier to growth, as it discourages stepping out of comfort zones and embracing new experiences. On the other hand, a growth mindset embraces the idea that abilities and intelligence can be developed through dedication and hard work. This perspective fosters a love for learning, resilience in the face of challenges, and a drive to improve. It's not just about effort, though; a growth mindset also involves a willingness to learn from criticism and the persistence to try different strategies when facing obstacles. Cultivating a growth mindset can lead to not only personal and professional achievements but also a more fulfilling and adventurous life.

A growth mindset, as opposed to a fixed mindset, fosters resilience and openness to new experiences. It encourages individuals and teams to view challenges as opportunities for learning, which can lead to innovation and improved performance. This mindset is instrumental in recognizing learning opportunities that contribute to broader objectives, such as revenue growth and customer acquisition.

Moreover, reframing setbacks as learning experiences can significantly enhance one's ability to bounce back from failures. Instead of self-criticism, analyzing what went wrong and extracting lessons from a failed job interview or a mistake can transform these events into valuable insights. This perspective shift not only aids in personal development but also cultivates a culture of learning and growth within an organization.

Interviews and the Internet

It's essential to maintain a positive outlook and view each interview as a learning experience. Even if you don't secure the job, every interview is an opportunity to refine your approach and understand the evolving dynamics of your industry. Keeping abreast of the latest trends and familiarizing yourself with the current terminology can give you a competitive edge. As companies invest more in employee training, staying informed and adaptable demonstrates your commitment to personal growth and professional development. This proactive attitude not only prepares you for future opportunities but also showcases your dedication to potential employers.

The concept of "value-added" results is about delivering work that stands out for its uniqueness and utility. It's the kind of contribution that resonates with employers and can be a decisive factor during interviews. This approach requires dedication and hard work, but the rewards are commensurate with the effort. By refusing to leave career progression to chance and instead taking proactive steps to excel, professionals can create opportunities for growth and recognition in their chosen fields.

In the professional realm, it's essential to maintain a growth mindset and resilience in the face of rejection. Rejection is not a reflection of personal failure but rather an opportunity for growth and improvement. It could be an indication to reassess one's presentation style, the content of the material, or the method of communication. A condescending delivery, even if unintended, can hinder the message from being well-received. True success is often the result of continuous effort, learning from feedback, and staying actively engaged in one's pursuits. Comfort zones are rarely the breeding grounds for success; instead, recognizing and leveraging one's strengths while being open to development can lead to significant achievements. Embracing this mindset is key to personal and professional development.

Making a conscious decision to think positively about oneself can lead to a more fulfilling and successful career path.

Before your interview, ensure you get a good night's sleep. Rehearse beforehand and prepare days in advance. Research the company and look up the interviewers on LinkedIn to understand their backgrounds. Establishing a morning and evening routine while unemployed can maximize your day's potential. Preparation leads to smoother days and a structured routine can offer more freedom. Being organized allows you to accomplish more, giving you the liberty to manage household chores and attend your children's sporting events. Remember, life doesn't just happen to you; your reactions to events are what can truly make a difference. The strategies outlined in my book are designed to enhance your overall freedom, providing a framework for a more organized and fulfilling life.

Interviews and the Internet

HR insider tip. *Preparing for a job interview is a critical step in the job search process. It's essential to bring extra copies of your cover letter and resume to the interview, as this shows organization and foresight. Researching the company and the interviewers on LinkedIn prior to your interview can provide valuable insight and common ground for building rapport. Finding shared experiences, such as previous employers or educational institutions, can be an excellent way to make a memorable connection.*

It is also crucial to dress professionally, regardless of the company's dress code, to convey a serious and respectful attitude toward the opportunity. Thorough preparation demonstrates to the HR recruiter and hiring manager that you are diligent and genuinely interested in the position, which can significantly influence their impression and decision-making. Remember: Being well-prepared can set you apart from other candidates and increase your chances of success.

Chapter 9:

Reflect on the Process

"But if we hope for that we see not, then do we with patience wait for it."

Romans 8:25

Just as documenting your goals and writing them down is a powerful tool, journaling is also powerful for personal development and self-care. It serves as a private canvas where one can express thoughts, emotions, and experiences without judgment.

By maintaining a consistent journaling routine, individuals create a space for regular reflection and mindfulness. This practice can lead to profound insights and a deeper understanding of one's thought patterns and behaviors

The act of writing in a journal allows for a momentary pause from the hustle of daily life, providing a sanctuary of tranquility where the mind can wander and explore. It's in these moments of solitude that one can truly connect with their inner self, fostering a sense of peace and clarity. The process of journaling can also serve as a cathartic release, helping to alleviate the burdens of stress and anxiety.

Journaling can be a vehicle for reinforcing one's strengths and aspirations. It encourages a shift in perspective, enabling individuals to focus on their achievements and the potential for future success rather than dwelling on past setbacks. This shift can naturally enhance one's optimism and overall outlook on life.

The mindfulness aspect of journaling is particularly impactful. It anchors individuals in the present moment, allowing them to engage fully with their current experiences and feelings. This practice of being "in the now" can heighten awareness and appreciation for life's nuances, often overlooked in the rush of day-to-day activities.

Additionally, journaling provides a platform for prob-

Reflect on the Process

lem-solving and critical thinking. It can be especially beneficial when dealing with life's challenges, such as job loss or personal failures. Writing about these experiences helps to process emotions and can lead to valuable lessons learned. It encourages a growth mindset, where obstacles are viewed as opportunities for learning and self-improvement.

In essence, journaling is more than just a method of self-expression; it's a journey of self-discovery and transformation. It's a commitment to oneself, a disciplined practice that nurtures the mind and soul. For those who embrace it, journaling can indeed be a transformative experience, leading to greater self-awareness, resilience, and joy.

In the relentless pursuit of the job search process and productivity, it's essential to remember the value of pausing and reflecting on life. This practice isn't merely a passive break from activity but a profound engagement with our experiences and thoughts. It allows us to appreciate the present, learn from the past, and make informed decisions for the future. Reflection can take many forms, from meditation and journaling to long walks or quiet contemplation. It's in these moments of stillness that we often find clarity and insight, leading to personal growth and a deeper understanding of our place in the world. By regularly taking time to pause and reflect, we cultivate a mindful approach to life, enhancing our well-being and enriching our life's journey.

Reflective journaling is a powerful tool for process improvement, offering a structured way to consider the efficacy of various methods and strategies. By taking the time to journal, one can delve into the nuances of what was effective and what fell short, providing a clear record that can be revisited and analyzed. This practice encourages a mindful approach to problem-solving, where each step of the process is evaluated for its contribution to the overall goal. It's an opportunity to celebrate successes, no matter how small, and to honestly assess and learn from what didn't work. Through this introspection, one can identify patterns, isolate variables that influence outcomes, and discern actionable insights for future endeavors.

Moreover, journaling can serve as a catalyst for innovation, prompting the exploration of alternative tactics and the refinement of existing procedures. It can also highlight areas where additional skills or knowledge may be required, guiding personal and professional development. By regularly engaging in this practice, individuals and teams can foster a culture of continuous improvement, where learning and adaptation are integral to success. Ultimately, the act of journaling not only aids in enhancing the process but also contributes to a deeper understanding of one's own learning and growth journey.

Journaling is a timeless practice cherished for its ability to capture thoughts, ideas, and experiences. While technology offers convenient solutions like audio journals and digital notes,

Reflect on the Process

the classic pen-and-paper method remains a beloved choice for many. The tactile sensation of writing, the physical act of turning pages, and the personal touch of a handwritten entry create a unique and intimate experience. A small, portable journal serves not only as a repository of thoughts but also as a constant companion, reflecting the owner's journey through life. It's a private space where plans can take shape, from redecorating a room to organizing personal spaces. The key is to approach journaling with intention, making it a deliberate part of one's routine rather than an afterthought. Whether it's setting aside time each day to write or carrying a journal throughout the house, the act of documenting one's life is a purposeful stride toward self-awareness and mindfulness. In this way, journaling transcends being a mere record of events; it becomes a canvas for the soul, where the mundane is transformed into the meaningful and every stroke of the pen is a step toward actualizing one's aspirations.

Starting a gratitude journal is a wonderful way to focus on the positive aspects of life and foster a sense of well-being. It can be a simple notebook or a dedicated app, but the key is consistency. Begin by setting aside a few minutes each day to reflect on moments or things that brought you joy, no matter how small. This could be a warm cup of coffee, a kind gesture from a stranger, or the comfort of your favorite book. As you write, try to relive the feelings of gratitude and happiness. Over time, you'll notice patterns of what consistently contributes to your happiness, which can be incredibly insightful. This practice not only boosts your mood in the present but also serves as a personal archive of positivity that you can look back on during challenging times. Remember, gratitude is like a muscle; the more you exercise it, the stronger it becomes, enhancing your overall perspective on life.

Your goals in life become clearer as you read and start to understand God's Word on a deeper level. As you spend time with God in prayer, talking to Him, and letting Him know your fears and concerns, you are becoming a new person. As it says in 2 Corinthians 5:17, you are a new creature in Christ. Through this process of obtaining gainful employment, a by-product of the job search journey is one of profound self-discovery. It's a time when one's aspirations and ambitions come into sharper focus, revealing what one truly seeks in their personal and professional life. This process of introspection and self-assessment can be enlightened by reading Scripture, God's Word, on a daily basis. This process of daily discipline often leads to a deeper understanding of one's values, strengths, and passions. As you navigate through the myriads of opportunities and challenges, each step taken is a move toward a clearer vision of your future. With every resume sent, interview attended, and feedback received, you're not just chasing a job; you're sculpting your destiny, aligning your career with your life's purpose. This path, though sometimes winding and uncertain, is a testament to the pursuit of fulfillment and happiness in one's work life. It's a reminder that the journey to-

Reflect on the Process

ward achieving your dreams is as significant as the destination itself.

The job search journey is indeed fraught with uncertainties and challenges that can test one's resilience. It's a process that not only evaluates one's skills and qualifications but also one's ability to adapt and learn from various situations. It's natural to reflect on interviews and interactions with potential employers, pondering on the "what ifs" and "could haves." However, it's crucial to recognize that such reflections should serve as learning experiences rather than sources of self-reproach.

Every interview is an opportunity to understand the dynamics of different workplaces and to hone one's interview skills. It's important to remember that not every job rejection is a reflection of one's abilities or worth. Many factors play into hiring decisions, including internal policies, budget constraints, and unforeseen organizational changes, which are beyond an applicant's control.

Instead of dwelling on the negatives, it's beneficial to focus on the positives, such as the experience gained and the insights learned about the industry and oneself. It's also helpful to maintain a proactive approach by continuing the job search, expanding one's network, and seeking feedback to improve future applications and interviews.

Embracing a mindset of growth and resilience can transform the job search from a daunting task into a journey of self-discovery and professional development. By letting go of the things one cannot change and focusing on the aspects one can influence, the job search becomes not just about finding a position but also about personal growth and preparing for the right opportunity when it arises.

In essence, the job search is a multifaceted experience that encompasses more than just the pursuit of employment. It's a period of introspection, skill enhancement, and, most importantly, learning to navigate the complexities of the professional world with grace and determination. The key is to keep moving forward, armed with the knowledge that each step, whether forward or backward, is a valuable part of the learning curve.

Navigating the job market can be a complex and often unpredictable journey. It's essential to approach each opportunity with a balance of preparation and adaptability. Reflecting on an interview experience is a valuable exercise, allowing one to consider areas for improvement such as preparation, company research, and understanding the interviewers' backgrounds. Yet, it's equally important to recognize factors beyond one's control, such as the interviewer's disposition or the company's internal dynamics.

Reflect on the Process

Asking oneself why a particular role or company is desirable is a critical step in aligning personal values and career aspirations. It's a reminder that the job search is not just about securing any position but about finding the right fit where one can thrive and contribute meaningfully. Life's experiences, including those in the professional realm, indeed serve as lessons that shape and refine our goals.

With each interview and interaction, clarity can emerge, revealing what one truly seeks in their career. This clarity is not just about the job itself but encompasses the environment, culture, and potential for growth. As one progresses through this process, it becomes apparent that every setback is a setup for a comeback, providing insights that guide future decisions.

The path to fulfilling one's dreams may not always be linear, but with persistence and introspection, it becomes more defined. Each step taken, whether it leads to an offer or not, is a building block in the construction of a career that resonates with one's deepest aspirations and values. In this journey, it's crucial to remember that not every outcome is within our control. It is our responses to these outcomes that shape our resilience, our perspective, and, ultimately, our success.

Prayer: try it—it works. It is an honor to pray to the Creator of the universe and thank Him for everything He has done for you. Bring with you a heart of gratitude for everything that He has done, all the "Red Seas" that He has parted in your life. God hears every prayer. Sometimes, we get impatient as we are waiting for a response. If we don't receive a response right away, we think that God must not have heard our prayer. I have always said that God has three responses to our prayers: (1) yes, (2) no, and (3) not yet. God knows best what we need and when we need it.

The Bible is often seen as a historical document, chronicling events from millennia ago. However, its enduring relevance lies in its philosophical and spiritual teachings, which many believe to be timeless. The concept of "the renewing of the mind" mentioned in the Bible speaks to a transformational process that is as pertinent today as it was centuries ago. It suggests a form of mental rejuvenation or reorientation that can lead to a more fulfilled and purposeful life.

In contemporary society, there is a tendency to seek out guidance on personal development and success. This is evident in the popularity of self-help literature focusing on financial success, career advancement, and early retirement. These books often provide strategies and principles that resonate with the readers' desires for achievement and prosperity. Yet, despite the practical advice these books offer, the fulfillment they promise can sometimes feel elusive after the last page is turned.

The Bible's approach to personal growth is less about material success and more about cultivating virtues like compassion,

Reflect on the Process

patience, and humility. It encourages introspection and moral inventory, promoting a holistic view of success that encompasses not just wealth and status but also character and community. The stories and parables within its pages are not just historical accounts but are meant to serve as allegories and lessons applicable to everyday life.

The transformative power of the Bible's teachings on the mind and spirit can be likened to the principles found in some self-help books. Both aim to guide individuals toward a better understanding of themselves and their place in the world. However, the Bible's emphasis on spiritual renewal offers a different dimension of self-improvement, one that encourages looking beyond the material and fostering a deeper connection with the transcendent.

In essence, the Bible invites readers to embark on a journey of self-discovery and spiritual awakening. It challenges one to reflect on their values, actions, and purpose. Through its narratives, it provides a framework for understanding human nature and the pursuit of a meaningful life. Whether one views it as a religious text or a compilation of wisdom literature, its potential to inspire and transform the mind remains a compelling aspect of its enduring legacy.

The Bible has been a cornerstone of spiritual guidance for countless individuals throughout history. Its teachings, parables, and narratives offer insights into moral and ethical living, providing a source of comfort and inspiration for many. The impact of the Bible extends beyond mere intellectual understanding; it reaches into the depths of the human heart, influencing values, shaping beliefs, and guiding actions. Its verses often resonate with personal significance, reflecting on the human experience and offering wisdom on life's most profound questions. Whether one approaches it as a religious text, a historical document, or a literary work, the Bible's influence on individual lives and broader culture is undeniable. It encourages introspection and personal growth, fostering a sense of connection with the divine and with the shared human journey. The Bible's role as a "how to" book is not just about following directives; it's about engaging with its teachings to cultivate a more compassionate, understanding, and fulfilling life.

Prayer, meditation, and reflective time hold significant importance in many individuals' lives due to their profound impact on mental, emotional, and spiritual well-being. These practices are often seen as pathways to greater peace, clarity, and connection with the divine or one's inner self. Prayer can be a means of communication with God, offering a way to express gratitude, seek guidance, or find comfort in times of distress. Prayer often involves quieting the mind, fostering a state of calm, and present-moment awareness. This can lead to increased awareness, mindfulness, and concentration. Reflective time allows for in-

Reflect on the Process

trospection, helping individuals align their job search actions with their job search values and goals. This helps an individual grow in wisdom and understanding. The practice of prayer can enhance one's sense of purpose, reduce stress, and contribute to overall happiness and contentment in life. They are tools that can help cultivate a balanced and centered approach to the complexities of everyday living.

The Bible has many, many scriptures in it that refer to the "renewing of your mind." The Bible has been regarded by many as a profound source of wisdom and guidance, transcending the typical categorization of literature. Its text, rich with historical narratives, parables, and teachings, has served as a cornerstone for personal growth and spiritual development for countless individuals throughout history. The principles contained within its pages offer insights into leading a life of virtue, navigating moral dilemmas, and finding solace during times of hardship. It is often turned to not just as a religious text but as a manual for living, providing counsel that many find applicable to a wide array of life's challenges. From the poetic reflections in Psalms to the sagacious Proverbs, the Bible encompasses a breadth of knowledge that continues to be relevant in contemporary society. Its influence is evident in the multitude of self-help books that draw upon its teachings, suggesting a timeless applicability to the human condition. Whether one approaches it for spiritual reasons or as a historical document, the Bible's impact on individual lives and collective culture is undeniable, affirming its place as a significant, if not the most significant, self-help book ever written.

The concept of renewing one's mind is deeply rooted in spiritual practices associated with transformative growth and personal development. It is a process that involves a conscious effort to shift one's thoughts and perspectives, aligning them with positive, life-affirming beliefs and values. This renewal is not a one-time event but a continuous journey throughout life of self-discovery and improvement. In limiting future growth, we must not accept complacency. By embracing this process, individuals can cultivate a mindset that fosters resilience, adaptability, and a deeper understanding of their purpose and potential. The renewed mind is thus a powerful catalyst for change, not only within oneself but also in the way one interacts with the world. It is about creating a new narrative for one's life, one that is guided by the wisdom of the Trinity, which provides compassion and an unwavering commitment to personal and spiritual growth combined.

God gives us free will and personal choice, which are central to many philosophical and ethical discussions. Free will is the idea that individuals have the power to make choices that are not predetermined by past events, genetics, or environment. It's a concept that suggests autonomy and self-determination, where a person's decisions are truly their own. Personal choice, on the

Reflect on the Process

other hand, refers to the selections individuals make among different options, reflecting their preferences, values, and beliefs. These choices can range from mundane daily decisions to life-altering commitments. Together, free will and personal choice form the bedrock of individual agency, the capacity of individuals to act independently and make their own free choices. This agency is often seen as a fundamental human right, underlying the ability to pursue a life that one finds meaningful and fulfilling. God's Word lights the path to pursuing and finding a life that has value, meaning, and purpose.

Others maintain that societal structures and inequalities limit the range of choices available to individuals, thus constraining personal freedom. Despite these debates, the belief in free will and personal choice remains a cornerstone of many legal systems and moral frameworks, which hold individuals responsible for their actions. It also inspires discussions on consent, autonomy, and the pursuit of happiness, which are vital to the fabric of modern society. As we navigate through life, the interplay of free will and personal choice continues to shape our identities, our societies, and our destinies.

While we are in the position of seeking employment, there is a balance between the concept of action versus inaction. Every action has a consequence, but it is equally true that inaction can be just as consequential. Choosing not to act is, in itself, a decision that can lead to a specific set of outcomes. For instance, in the context of the job search process and personal growth, not applying for one more job or not taking the time to update your resume can actually result in stagnation with your job search goals. Not taking the initiative to learn, do better, and move above and beyond the action you would normally take can result in stagnation.

In a professional setting, failing to adapt to changes or take on new challenges may lead to missed opportunities and could potentially harm a career. Similarly, in relationships, not communicating or addressing issues can create distances and misunderstandings.

The ripple effects of doing nothing can be far-reaching, affecting not just the individual but the people around you. It's important to recognize that we are not powerless; even small actions can have significant impact. Whether it's through speaking up, lending a hand, or simply choosing to learn something new, our actions contribute to shaping our reality. The key is to be mindful of our choices and the potential effects they carry, understanding that the path of inaction is a choice with its own set of consequences. Ultimately, it's through our actions that we express our values, aspirations, and commitment to ourselves and the world within and around us.

The concept of "letting go" can be a profound practice in life, particularly when it comes to the outcomes we desire. It's a paradoxical truth that, often, the tighter we cling to our hopes and plans and the more control we seek, the more elusive they become. This is not to say that one should not have goals or strive for success, but rather that the fixation on a specific outcome can lead to a counterproductive mindset. When we release the grip of control and keep an open mind, we open ourselves to a broader range of possibilities, allowing for more natural progression and, often, more satisfying results.

Letting go involves trust—not just in the unpredictability of life but also in ourselves and that God is with us every step of the way. We rely on the Trinity—the Holy Trinity—to help us adapt and thrive in changing circumstances. It's about understanding that control is often an illusion and that, by trying to enforce it, we may actually be limiting our own potential. By surrendering control, we can find a sense of peace and acceptance, which, ironically, can lead to a greater sense of peace and success in our lives.

Relying on God does not advocate passivity; rather, it encourages active engagement with life in a more flexible and open-minded manner. It's about going to the Holy Trinity for help, doing our best, and then stepping back and letting the natural course of events unfold. This can be particularly liberating when facing situations that are truly beyond our control, such as the actions of others or the outcomes of well-intentioned efforts. Our steps are guided by the Holy Spirit. We need to pray, listen, be at peace, and take time for reflection.

In essence, letting go is an exercise in humility and wisdom. It's recognizing that, despite our best efforts, there are factors in life that we cannot predict or command. It's a shift from a mindset of scarcity and fear to one of abundance and confidence. By letting go, we allow life to flow, we reduce stress and anxiety, and we position ourselves to recognize and seize opportunities that we might otherwise overlook.

Ultimately, letting go is about embracing the journey of life with all its twists and turns. A friend of mine reminds me during difficult circumstances that, "God is in control." It's about living in the moment, appreciating the present, and having faith that, regardless of what the future holds, we have the resilience and resourcefulness to navigate it. It's a powerful practice that can lead to personal growth, inner peace, and a deeper connection with the world around us.

In searching for employment, whether we are college students, stay-at-home moms, or seasoned executives, the human need for validation and feeling valued is deeply rooted in our psychological makeup. This need for validation is not just a desire but a crucial element of human interaction that fosters connection and mutual respect. It's linked to our basic needs for love and belonging.

Reflect on the Process

Validation serves as a confirmation that our thoughts, feelings, and actions are acknowledged and accepted by others. It can be a powerful tool in building self-confidence and a sense of security. In the workplace, for instance, validation from managers and peers is essential for creating a positive environment where employees feel appreciated and motivated. The absence of validation in such settings can lead to dissatisfaction and a lack of engagement.

The interesting process of validation is not only about receiving approval but also about giving approval to others. It humanizes us, allowing for empathy and understanding to flourish in our relationships. When we validate others, we communicate that we value their perspective and recognize their contributions, which can strengthen bonds and promote a more supportive community.

In conclusion, the need for validation is a natural and healthy part of being human. God created us, loves us, values us, and, most of all, desires a relationship with us. He is waiting for us to reach out to Him. Understanding the need for this relationship with our God, our Creator, leads to a more fulfilling and harmonious life within ourselves and with others.

HR insider tip. *Reflecting on each step of the job search and interview process is a valuable practice. It allows you to identify your strengths and areas for improvement. Even when positive feedback is received, such as being told by the HR recruiter that you are the most qualified candidate, it is important to remain measured and considerate in your response. Having a potential start date in mind shows preparedness, but also ensure it allows for adequate personal time before commencing a new role. Confidence is key. It's essential to maintain it throughout the job search process, even after an offer is extended. Until you officially start the position, continue to approach the job market with diligence and optimism.*

Chapter 10:
Keep an Open Mind

"I hear counsel, receive instruction, and accept correction that I may be wise in the time to come."

Proverbs 19:20 (paraphrased)

Developing or keeping an open mind requires a willingness to venture beyond the familiar and explore the uncharted. It's about challenging the status quo and daring to imagine the possibilities that lie outside learned behaviors or conventional ways of thinking. This approach is not just about being different for the sake of it but about seeking out fresh perspectives and novel solutions that can lead to breakthroughs in any field. Whether it's spiritual, art, science, business, or technology, thinking outside the box can lead to discoveries that reshape our understanding and expand our horizons. A mindset that values curiosity, encourages risk-taking, and celebrates the Holy Spirit drives progress and inspires change.

Self-development and change present challenges, and these can feel amplified during periods of unemployment, making a career change, or advancing your career. However, these challenges offer a unique opportunity to focus on personal and spiritual growth along with skill enhancement. Using this time in your life to brush up on existing skills or learn new ones can make an individual more marketable. Seeking self-improvement is a skill that employers seek in a candidate as it builds a strong foundation for future career moves. Additionally, advancing education, whether through formal degrees, certifications, or online courses, significantly boosts one's profile. It's also a time to explore personal interests that may have been sidelined due to work commitments, such as hobbies or volunteer work, which can enrich one's personal life and sometimes lead to unexpected career paths. Maintaining a structured schedule, optimizing online profiles, and developing a personal website or portfolio are also proactive steps that can be taken. Starting a side hustle not only keeps one engaged but also opens up new avenues for income and skill development.

Updating resumes and cover letters, researching potential employers, and preparing for interviews are essential tasks that can be done to prepare for any re-entry into the workforce. It's important to remember that seeking employment can be a stressful and uncertain time; however, it can also be a period of significant personal development and a chance to redirect one's career in a positive direction.

Some important advice that I have provided job seekers based on my own spiritual growth and job search activities is to watch the words you speak over yourself and your life. Remember to say only positive things about your job search, no matter what your current job status or situation is. No matter how difficult it may be, stay away from saying negative things to yourself, and especially refrain from saying negative things about your life or the job search process out loud.

As we are reminded in Proverbs 18:21, "Death and life are in the power of the tongue: and they that love it shall eat the fruit thereof." In other words, we will bear the consequences of what we say with the use of our words. What you say can preserve your life or destroy it. Your "words have power." Try this experiment: for one week, make it a goal not to say anything negative to anyone—your spouse, best friend, neighbor, pastor—whoever it may be. Try this for one week and take notice of what has happened. Notice the change in how you feel and in the behavior of others. Are you more pleasant to be around? Are you receiving more positive news? More job opportunities? More job offers? Accept the consequences of your words, as you will witness the profound impact that language and communication have on your human experience.

Words can inspire, soothe a grieving heart, provoke laughter, and even change the course of history. They carry the weight of our intentions and the breadth of our emotions, capable of bridging gaps between cultures and generations. The right words at the right time can uplift, educate, and empower, while the wrong ones can cause irreparable harm. In Proverbs 15:1 it states, "A soft answer turns away wrath, but grievous words stir up anger." How do people feel when they are around you? This is a good indicator of either your positive or negative outlook on life. Responsibility comes with the spoken and written word. In everyday interactions, the power of words is ever-present, shaping our realities and the world we share. It's a reminder that with this God-given gift comes the duty to use it wisely and to communicate with clarity, compassion, and respect for the profound influence our words can have.

Words are indeed a powerful reflection of our inner thoughts, serving as a bridge between the intangible realm of the mind and the tangible outer world. They allow us to express a range of emotions, articulate complex ideas, and share our deepest beliefs and desires. The process of transforming thought into language is a remarkable aspect of human cognition, enabling us to convey not just information but also the nuances of our individual perspectives. Through words, we can influence others, shape narratives, and leave a lasting impact on society. They are the tools with which we construct our realities, negotiate our relationships, and navigate the myriad experiences of life. Whether spoken or written, words carry the weight of our intentions and are the vessels of our creativity. Words are instruments for our interactions and the legacy of our intellectual endeavors. In essence, words are the manifestation of our inner selves, intricately woven into the fabric of our shared human experience.

Words also affect our relationships with others; however, our words also affect our relationship with ourselves. The intricate relationship between our inner thoughts and the outer world is a profound one, deeply rooted in the psychological and philosophical understanding of human existence. Our inner thought life, composed of our beliefs, attitudes, and self-talk, can significantly influence our external reality. Positive self-talk, for instance, has the power to boost confidence and reduce stress, leading to more favorable interactions and outcomes in the outer world. Conversely, negative self-talk can hinder performance and lead to increased stress or anxiety, affecting our behavior and the way others perceive us.

The concept of the "inner self" plays a pivotal role in this dynamic. It encompasses our subconscious thoughts, memories, emotions, and desires—the very essence of our identity. When we are in tune with our inner self, we can navigate life with greater authenticity and purpose, aligning our actions with our true intentions. This alignment can manifest in improved relationships, better decision-making, and a more fulfilling life experience.

Moreover, the process of introspection and self-awareness allows us to recognize and modify our internal dialogue. By fostering an analytical and future-oriented self-talk, we can set the stage for personal growth and positive change. This inner transformation can then ripple outwards, influencing our external circumstances and interactions.

It's also important to consider the biases that our inner thoughts create. These biases shape our interpretation of external events and can affect our judgment and behavior, leading to both positive and negative outcomes. By working to mitigate the negative impact of our inner thoughts, we can approach the world with a clearer and more objective perspective. We need to stay open and work to mitigate any impact from negative thoughts that affect our judgment and behavior.

Keep an Open Mind

The inner changes we cultivate within ourselves can gradually affect our outer life. Our behavior, the way we act, and how we respond to situations can change, thereby affecting our relationships and the experiences we undergo. This reflection of our internal state of mind in our external environment underscores the power of our thoughts and the importance of nurturing a positive, resilient inner life.

Building an inside-out life, where the inner self informs and harmonizes with the outer self, is essential for achieving a balanced and fulfilling existence. It provides the moral core and centeredness necessary for discerning what aspects of the outer world to engage with and how to deal with the consequences of those engagements. Ultimately, understanding and managing the interplay between our inner thought life and the outer world is key to personal development and well-being.

In addition to monitoring our inner thoughts and working on staying positive, be aware of negative people in your life. You may also have noticed these individuals as "dream stealers." You come up with a creative idea or an idea to open up a new business of your own, and there is the subtle (or not so subtle) put down. That is, there could be people in your life who are unhappy with themselves and take it out on you. It's important to recognize that people may intentionally or unintentionally provide a negative response to your new job, business, or career idea. Often, the most significant barriers are the ones we impose on ourselves.

Keep in mind that there may be external factors, such as negative individuals who may doubt or belittle one's ambitions. However, there may be internal factors in ourselves, such as self-doubt and fear of failure. Here are a few examples of self-talk that may be keeping you from taking a risk and fulfilling your dreams and goals:

- *Self-talk:* "I won't get a new job because I'm too young, too old, I'm over 50…"

- ✓ *Change mindset or thought process to:* "I'll get a new job because of all my wisdom, knowledge, and experience that I can bring to my new employer."

- *Self-talk:* "I can't figure this out. I'm not smart enough. I don't have enough experience or education."

- ✓ *Change mindset or thought process to:* "I've been in difficult situations before and have figured things out. I am resourceful, smart, and kind."

Overcoming these challenges requires a strong sense of self-belief and the determination to persevere despite setbacks. Surrounding oneself with supportive and like-minded individuals can also provide the encouragement needed to push through the negativity and continue striving toward one's goals. Ultimately, identifying and addressing the presence of dream stealers in one's life is a crucial step in the journey to personal and professional fulfillment.

It takes courage to live the life of your dreams. Living life with courage is a powerful affirmation of one's own existence as it involves embracing the unknown, taking risks, and stepping out of comfort zones. Pray bold prayers. In Proverbs 28:1 (NIV) it reads, "The righteous are as bold as a lion." As a representation of strength in Scripture, the lion exemplifies unwavering power and fortitude.

Courage and strength are not the absence of fear but rather the determination to move forward in spite of it. It's about making choices that align with one's true self, values, and aspirations. Courageous living means acknowledging vulnerabilities and facing challenges head-on, whether they are personal, professional, or social. It's about having the strength to be authentic and the resilience to recover from setbacks. This kind of bravery can lead to a life that is not only lived but also cherished and full of purpose. It inspires others and often leads to a ripple effect, encouraging more people to live boldly and without regret. The courage to live your life fully is a testament to the human spirit's ability to overcome, to thrive, and to find joy in the journey of life.

Understanding cause and effect is crucial in various fields, such as business, science, history, and economics, where it is used to explain or predict outcomes and make informed decisions. For instance, in science, observing the effects of certain actions or conditions allows researchers to hypothesize about the underlying causes. Similarly, historians may analyze events to understand the causes that led to significant historical outcomes. In economics, cause and effect can be seen in the way market forces interact, with supply and demand driving prices and production.

Moreover, the concept extends beyond academic disciplines and into everyday life, where understanding the consequences of our actions can lead to better decision-making. For example, if one understands that eating unhealthy food can cause health problems, they may choose to adopt a healthier diet. Likewise, recognizing that hard work often leads to success can motivate individuals to put forth greater effort in their endeavors.

However, identifying cause and effect can sometimes be complex, as multiple factors often contribute to a single outcome. This complexity can lead to misunderstandings or oversimplifications, as people may attribute an effect to a single cause when, in reality, it is the result of a confluence of factors. For example, economic downturns are rarely the result of a single event but are usually the culmination of various economic, political, and social factors.

Keep an Open Mind

In literature and storytelling, cause and effect are used to create narrative tension and drive plot development. Characters' actions (causes) have consequences (effects) that propel the story forward, often leading to conflict and resolution. This dynamic is what keeps readers engaged as they anticipate the outcomes of the characters' decisions and actions.

In the realm of philosophy, cause and effect are also subjects of deep contemplation. Philosophers have long debated the nature of causality, questioning whether causes truly precede effects or if our perception of this sequence is merely a construct of the human mind. Some have even pondered the implications of cause and effect on concepts like free will and determinism.

In conclusion, the principle of cause and effect is a cornerstone of human understanding, providing a framework for interpreting the world around us. It helps us make sense of the past, navigate the present, and anticipate the future. While it may not always be straightforward, its significance in shaping the course of events and human behavior cannot be overstated. As we continue to explore and analyze the causes and effects that govern our lives, we gain deeper insights into the intricate workings of the universe and our place within it.

Reading the Bible will change the way you think and help you see things differently in life. Change your mindset. Change how you view things.

The VIP Job Search

In Romans 12:2 (ESV), Scripture tells us about one essential means of transformation—"the renewal of your mind." The Bible, when read and studied, will help you think differently and more successfully as you are reading God's instruction book for life. The Bible's distinction as one of the most widely read books in the world is indeed well-documented, with Guinness World Records recognizing it as the best-selling book of all time, boasting an estimated 5 billion copies sold and distributed. Its profound influence on literature, culture, and individual lives is undeniable. However, its status as a frequently misunderstood text is equally notable. Misinterpretations can arise from a variety of factors, including cultural and historical distance from the original texts, translation discrepancies, and the complex nature of its various literary genres. Common misconceptions include treating the Bible as a monolithic text with a single genre or intention rather than a collection of diverse writings encompassing history, poetry, prophecy, and more. Additionally, verses taken out of context can lead to misunderstandings about the Bible's messages. For instance, some may interpret the Bible as a rulebook or a source of direct, personal messages, while others might point to perceived contradictions or inaccuracies without considering the nuances of textual criticism and hermeneutics. The challenge for readers is to approach the Bible with an understanding of its historical and cultural backdrop, recognizing the intent of its human authors and the divine inspiration attributed to it by believers. Engaging with scholarly resources and interpretations can also provide clarity and prevent common pitfalls in understanding this ancient and complex text.

The perspective that difficulties in life are opportunities is a testament to the resilient human spirit. It's a viewpoint that transforms challenges into stepping stones for growth rather than obstacles that impede progress. This mindset is often the hallmark of successful individuals who have learned to embrace adversity and extract wisdom from it. It's not just about being optimistic; it's about being strategic and proactive in the face of life's inevitable hurdles.

Every difficulty carries with it the seeds of an equivalent or greater benefit; every adversity contains the potential for equal or greater success. Hope that is found in reading God's Word encourages individuals to look beyond the immediate discomfort and to see the potential for personal development and innovation.

For instance, economic recessions, while challenging, can lead to new markets and business models. Personal failures can lead to introspection and a renewed focus on one's life goals and changing or improving strategies. Even in the natural world, ecosystems adapt and evolve in response to environmental stressors, leading to increased resilience and diversity.

In the professional realm, difficulties often drive innovation. Companies that face challenges head-on, adapting to new technologies and changing market conditions, often emerge stronger. They develop new strategies, products, and services that not only solve their immediate problems but also set them apart from the competition.

On a personal level, overcoming difficulties can lead to a deeper understanding of oneself and one's capabilities. It can build character, foster resilience, and cultivate empathy for others facing similar challenges. It's through overcoming difficulties that people often discover their true passions and the drive to pursue them.

Viewing difficulties as opportunities is a powerful paradigm shift that can lead to significant personal and professional growth. It's a mindset that doesn't diminish the reality of hardship but instead focuses on the potential for positive outcomes. It's about finding the silver lining, learning from every situation, and using those lessons to move forward more intelligently and effectively.

Embracing a mindset of innovation requires a willingness to venture beyond the familiar and explore the uncharted. It's about challenging the status quo and daring to imagine the possibilities that lie outside conventional boundaries. This approach is not just about being different for the sake of it but about seeking out fresh perspectives and novel solutions that can lead to breakthroughs in any field. Whether it's in art, science, business, or technology, thinking outside the box can lead to discoveries that reshape our understanding and expand our horizons. It's a mindset that values curiosity, encourages risk-taking, and celebrates the creative spirit that drives progress and inspires change.

Being unemployed for an extended period, such as a year, can be a challenging experience, but there are proactive steps one can take to navigate this situation. It's important to use the time to develop skills relevant to the job market.

In summary:

- ✓ Engaging in online courses, volunteer work, or even part-time jobs can enhance one's resume and keep skills sharp.
- ✓ Networking is also crucial; attending industry meetups, joining professional groups, or connecting with peers online can open new opportunities.
- ✓ Preparing job materials, such as a tailored resume and cover letter, is essential, and one should be ready to explain employment gaps positively, focusing on personal growth and skill development during the period.
- ✓ Investing in education, whether formal or informal, can also be beneficial, as it shows a commitment to continuous learning and adaptability.

- ✓ Mental health is equally important; seeking support from friends, family, or professionals can help maintain a positive outlook.
- ✓ Lastly, setting a routine and staying active can contribute to a sense of purpose and well-being during the job search process.

The steps outlined above, combined with persistence and a positive attitude, can significantly improve the chances of employment. Whether it is re-entering the workforce, obtaining gainful employment, or advancing in your chosen career, the path must be clear and in focus.

Maintaining an open mind is a fundamental aspect of personal growth and career progress. It allows individuals to consider different perspectives, embrace new ideas, and adapt to change. Open-mindedness is not just about accepting different viewpoints; it's about actively seeking them out and considering them thoughtfully. This quality fosters innovation and creativity, as it encourages people to look beyond their preconceived notions and explore new possibilities. In a world that is constantly evolving, the ability to remain open to new concepts and adapt accordingly is invaluable.

Open-mindedness also plays a crucial role in interpersonal relationships and communication. It enables individuals to engage in meaningful dialogues, where ideas can be exchanged and

Keep an Open Mind

understood rather than dismissed or debated contentiously. This approach can lead to more harmonious interactions and a deeper understanding of others. Furthermore, open-mindedness is linked to critical thinking and problem-solving skills. By being willing to consider various angles and solutions, as found in the job-search process, keeping an open mind may help individuals navigate complex situations more effectively.

In the realm of education, an open mind is essential for learning and intellectual development. It allows students to absorb new information, question existing knowledge, and synthesize diverse ideas. This mindset is equally important in the professional world, where it can lead to better decision-making and leadership. Leaders who are open-minded are better equipped to anticipate future trends, respond to challenges, and guide their organizations toward success.

Open-mindedness encourages empathy and understanding. Adopting a flexible mindset and being open to new ideas and perspectives is crucial in a rapidly evolving world. It allows individuals and societies to adapt to change, innovate, and solve complex problems. Being stubborn or closed-minded can hinder personal growth and limit one's ability to fully engage with the diverse and multifaceted nature of life. It's important to cultivate curiosity and a willingness to consider different viewpoints, as this can lead to a deeper understanding of the world and the people in it. Embracing new concepts and ways of thinking can enrich one's experiences and contribute to a more harmonious and dynamic existence.

In conclusion, the importance of keeping an open mind cannot be overstated. It is a trait that enhances personal development, fosters positive relationships, and drives progress in various aspects of life. Cultivating an open-minded approach can lead to a richer, more fulfilling experience, both personally and collectively.

HR insider tip. *Identifying and understanding one's transferable skills is a crucial step in career development. It enables individuals to broaden their job search and consider roles that they may not have previously contemplated, thus opening doors to new possibilities and career growth. Exploring new career opportunities in unfamiliar industries can be a rewarding venture. It allows for the application of transferable skills, which are valuable assets that can be adapted to various job roles. These skills, such as leadership, communication, problem-solving, and teamwork, are not industry-specific and can be leveraged to excel in a diverse range of positions.*

Chapter 11:

Landing the Job

"I always pray; I don't faint, quit, or give up!"

Luke 18:1 (paraphrased)

Congratulations! You have been offered a new job. This is a significant milestone, marking the beginning of a fresh chapter filled with opportunities for growth and learning. This new career path is exciting and commendable. It's time to bring all your experiences, skills, and enthusiasm into a new environment where you can contribute to your new role with a unique perspective. This transition often comes with mixed emotions of excitement and nervousness as you step into unfamiliar territory, ready to face new challenges and build new relationships.

It's an opportunity to set new goals and work towards achieving them, continuously expanding your expertise and professional network. As you navigate this journey, remember to embrace the changes, stay adaptable, and keep an open mind to the possibilities that lie ahead.

You're taking forward the valuable lessons from your past experiences. These lessons are the stepping stones to success, providing insights and wisdom that can guide decision-making and strategies in your new role. Remember, every challenge faced and obstacle overcome has contributed to your growth, equipping you with resilience and adaptability. As you progress towards your goals, these lessons will serve as a compass, helping you navigate through the complexities of your new job with confidence and foresight.

Your new career path is not just a job change; it's a chance to redefine your professional identity and leave a lasting impact in your field. Congratulations on this new beginning, and may it lead you to success and fulfillment.

Securing your first job after college graduation or after a prolonged period of joblessness can be a daunting task. However, with a strategic approach, it is entirely achievable. The key is to focus on enhancing your skills, which can be done through various online courses or volunteer work that adds value to your resume. Networking plays a crucial role; attending job fairs, joining professional groups, or even volunteering can lead to valuable connections. It's also essential to have your job materials, such as your resume and cover letter, updated and tailored to the positions you're applying for. Investing in further education can also be beneficial, as it demonstrates a commitment to personal and professional growth. Remember to be patient and persistent, as the job search process can take time. It's important to stay positive and keep your skills sharp, ensuring that when the right opportunity comes along, you're ready to seize it.

Here are a few things you have learned during your job search process:

- You learned to take one day at a time.
- You learned about time management.
- You learned how to balance your career objectives, with time for relaxation.
- You learned that both you and God are a majority.
- You learned that your future is in God's hands.
- You learned to walk closer to God.
- You learned about your relationship with God.
- You learned more about God's character and who He really is.

Being unemployed for an extended period of time, searching for an advanced level in your career, or looking for your first job can all be challenging experiences. However, there are proactive steps one can take to navigate this situation. It's important to use the time to develop skills relevant to the job market. Investing in education, whether formal or informal, can also be beneficial, as it shows a commitment to continuous learning and adaptability. Setting a routine and staying active can contribute to a greater sense of purpose. Persistence and a positive attitude significantly improve the chances of re-entering the workforce and obtaining employment.

There is also prayer. Prayer holds a place of great significance in many people's lives, serving as a profound and personal way to connect with God. It is a means to foster a closer relationship with God, allowing individuals to express gratitude, seek guidance, and find comfort in times of distress. Prayer can also be a source of strength, offering solace and a sense of peace that transcends understanding. It is a practice that aligns our will with that of God's, helping us to navigate the complexities of life with a sense of purpose and direction. The act of prayer is a universal expression of hope, a testament to the enduring human spirit seeking connection and meaning in the vast tapestry of existence.

A significant concern in today's modern economy is job stability. Companies may relocate, merge, or restructure for various reasons, including financial benefits, market expansion, or strategic partnerships. Outsourcing has also become a common practice as businesses seek cost-effective solutions. These changes can lead to job displacement, but they also create opportunities for growth and diversification of skills. It's beneficial for professionals to continuously develop their skill set, stay adaptable, and network within their industry to navigate these changes successfully. Proactive career management and lifelong learning are key strategies to maintain employability in a dynamic job market.

Whether you have endured a job loss, did not receive a promotion you were hoping for, or are looking to re-enter the job market, each situation can be a significant life event. It's essential to reflect on the experience to glean valuable insights. It's an opportunity to reassess one's career path, identify strengths and weaknesses, and develop new strategies for future job stability. Learning from such an experience can involve understanding industry trends, improving professional skills, and expanding one's network. It's also a chance to evaluate personal financial planning and discover ways to build a more resilient economic foundation. Ultimately, the lessons learned from a job loss can lead to personal growth, better job preparedness, and a more robust approach to navigating one's career journey.

Choosing to continue working despite the option of early retirement is a decision that many face. It's a personal choice that can be influenced by a variety of factors, such as financial readiness, the desire for continued professional engagement, or simply the love for one's job. Your decision to stay in the workforce reflects a commitment to your career and an acknowledgment of the value that your experience brings. It's a commendable choice that underscores the importance of personal fulfillment in one's professional journey.

Creating a life-long, permanent plan in today's job market requires a multifaceted approach. It's essential to continuously develop skills that are in demand, such as critical thinking, problem-solving, and adaptability. Networking and building professional relationships can also open doors to opportunities that may not be widely advertised. Additionally, embracing lifelong learning and staying updated with industry trends can make one more attractive to potential employers. It's also beneficial to cultivate a personal brand that reflects one's skills, values, and professional experiences, making it easier to stand out in a competitive job market. Lastly, considering alternative career paths or entrepreneurial ventures could provide a more controlled and self-directed professional journey.

Creating a comprehensive life plan is a profound step towards personal development and fulfillment. Start by envisioning your ideal future without constraints, considering all aspects of life, such as career, personal growth, relationships, and health. Write down specific, measurable, achievable, relevant, and time-bound (SMART) goals. Reflect on the lessons you've learned so far and how they can shape your decisions moving forward. Consider the skills you need to develop and the habits you want to cultivate. Remember, this plan is not set in stone; it's a living document that should evolve as you grow and learn. It's also important to celebrate small victories along the way to keep motivated. By applying the lessons of the past and maintaining a clear vision for the future, you can create a roadmap that leads to a fulfilling life.

Growth and transformation are often the results of challenging experiences. The journey of self-discovery can lead to profound insights about one's intrinsic value, which transcends external measures such as job titles or salaries. Embracing this process can lead to a stronger sense of self and a deeper understanding of one's purpose and potential. It's important to hold onto the lessons learned, as they are invaluable in continuing to navigate life's journey with resilience and authenticity. Remembering that change is a constant part of life can help one remain adaptable and open to new experiences that foster further growth.

Embracing one's authentic self is the cornerstone of genuine success. It's about aligning one's actions with inner values and convictions rather than conforming to external expectations. This authenticity serves as a guide, allowing individuals to utilize their unique gifts, talents, and abilities in service to others. Reflecting on one's legacy prompts a deeper consideration of the impact one wishes to leave on the world. Life's imperfections and challenges are not endpoints but rather opportunities for growth and learning. Remember, setbacks are a part of the journey that offer lessons that contribute to your personal development and resilience.

In summary, obtaining employment requires a comprehensive approach that includes skill development, networking, preparation of job materials, interview practice, market research, realistic goal-setting, and seeking professional support. With dedication and a proactive attitude, individuals can successfully navigate the path to re-employment and embark on a fulfilling career journey.

The journey of mothers returning to work is a multifaceted one, encompassing the excitement of re-engaging with professional life and the challenges of balancing work and family responsibilities. Organizations are increasingly recognizing the value that mothers bring to the workforce, not only in terms of their professional skills but also the unique perspectives and life experiences they offer. There are programs that provide the necessary support and training to help mothers bridge the gap between career breaks and re-entry into the professional world. These programs often include personalized training plans, mentorship, and strategic diversity programs, which are crucial for refreshing skills and boosting confidence.

Moreover, the rise of back-to-work programs reflects a growing awareness of the untapped potential within this demographic. With 43 percent of highly qualified women having left work voluntarily at some point, there's a significant pool of talent eager to return. These programs not only aid in skill enhancement but also in addressing the resume gap, which is often a major concern for returning mothers. By providing opportunities for cross-functional collaboration and mentorship, such initiatives can significantly ease the transition back to work.

Companies are beginning to understand the importance of work-life integration and are implementing policies that respect this balance. This includes offering flexible work arrangements, management and leadership training, and other benefits that cater to the needs of working mothers. Such measures not only facilitate the return of mothers to the workforce but also contribute to a more diverse and inclusive work environment.

In addition to structured programs, the role of community and peer support cannot be overstated. Networks of working mothers can provide invaluable advice, share resources, and offer moral support. The collective wisdom and shared experiences within these communities serve as a powerful resource for those navigating the complexities of re-entering the workforce.

The narrative of mothers returning to work is changing, with society beginning to value and support their contributions more than ever. As more companies and organizations recognize the need for and benefits of such support, the path for returning mothers will become less daunting. The collective efforts of dedicated programs, supportive workplaces, and empowering communities are creating a new paradigm where the professional aspirations of mothers are not just recognized but actively facilitated. This shift not only benefits the individuals involved but also enriches the workforce with diverse experiences and viewpoints, ultimately contributing to a more dynamic and innovative business landscape.

Retirees often seek part-time employment for various reasons, including the desire to supplement their income and maintain social interactions. Indeed, part-time work can offer a flexible schedule, allowing retirees to enjoy their retirement while still engaging in the workforce. Opportunities range from roles that leverage a retiree's extensive work experience and skills to those that may involve learning new abilities or exploring different interests. Positions such as merchandisers, housekeepers, secretaries, and seasonal retail associates are commonly available and can provide both financial benefits and a sense of community and purpose. Additionally, organizations like AARP offer resources and job listings tailored to retirees seeking part-time work, recognizing the value and experience they bring to the workplace. It's also worth noting that part-time jobs can contribute to a retiree's overall well-being by keeping them mentally and physically active, which is an important aspect of a healthy retirement lifestyle.

Graduating college students looking to secure full-time employment can enhance their job prospects by engaging in a variety of strategic activities. Gaining relevant experience through internships or part-time jobs is crucial, as it demonstrates practical skills and a commitment to the field. Networking is another key step; building relationships with professionals and alumni in the industry can lead to opportunities that are not publicly advertised. It's also important to research the job market to understand the demand for certain roles and the skills required.

Students should be proactive in their job search, attending career fairs and utilizing their college's career services for resume reviews and interview preparation. Creating a professional online presence, particularly on platforms like LinkedIn, can attract potential employers and showcase a student's skills and experiences. Additionally, maintaining a well-crafted resume, tailored for each application and optimized for Application Tracking Systems, can increase the chances of getting noticed.

Volunteering and participating in clubs or organizations can also enrich a student's resume, providing evidence of leadership and teamwork abilities. For those in creative fields, building a portfolio website to display their work can be beneficial. Taking online courses and acquiring new skills relevant to their desired industry can make a graduate more competitive. Finding a mentor to offer guidance and support throughout the job search process can provide invaluable insights and advice.

Graduates should be prepared to work hard and be persistent in their job search, as it can take several months to secure a position. By combining these efforts, graduates can improve their employability and increase their chances of finding fulfilling full-time employment after college. It's a process that requires dedication, adaptability, and a willingness to continuously learn and grow professionally.

Professionals looking to advance in their careers can adopt a multifaceted approach to ensure growth and development. Setting clear, long-term goals is a fundamental step, as it provides direction and motivation. Researching various career paths and understanding the qualifications required for advancement can help in creating a strategic plan. Networking plays a crucial role in career advancement; building a strong professional network can open doors to new opportunities and insights. Seeking mentorship is also beneficial, as mentors can offer guidance, support, and valuable industry knowledge.

Continuing education and acquiring new skills are essential for staying relevant in an ever-evolving job market. Professionals should be proactive in seeking out leadership opportunities, as these experiences can demonstrate their capability to handle higher responsibilities. Volunteering for projects outside of one's comfort zone can also be a way to showcase initiative and learn new skills. Conducting informational interviews with individuals in desired positions can provide a realistic view of the necessary steps for advancement.

Maintaining a professional demeanor, being punctual, and dressing appropriately can positively influence one's professional image. It's important to be adaptable and open to change, as the path to career advancement may require shifts in roles or industries. Staying updated with industry trends and technological advancements ensures that one's skills do not become obsolete. Finally, it's crucial to communicate one's career aspirations with supervisors to align personal goals with organizational objectives, which can lead to mutually beneficial outcomes.

Advancing in a career requires a combination of goal setting, continuous learning, networking, mentorship, and professional development. By actively engaging in these practices, professionals can enhance their prospects for career growth and achieve their professional aspirations.

Re-entering the job market can be a significant milestone,

marking a new chapter in one's professional journey. It often requires a strategic approach, starting with a focused job search that aligns with one's skills, interests, and values. Refreshing one's resume is a critical step, ensuring it reflects current skills and experiences relevant to the desired industry. It's also beneficial to showcase skills, particularly those developed or honed during the employment gap, as they can be a testament to continuous personal and professional growth. Describing the period away from the job market effectively can turn a potential drawback into a compelling narrative of resilience and dedication. Networking remains a powerful tool, allowing individuals to reconnect with former colleagues and meet new professionals in their field. Engaging with industry-specific groups and attending professional events can open doors to opportunities that may not be widely advertised. Additionally, leveraging technology and online platforms can amplify one's presence in the job market, making it easier to discover and apply for positions. For some, starting with part-time or temporary work can be a practical way to ease back into the workforce, providing valuable experience and potential pathways to full-time employment. It's essential to remain open to new experiences and learning opportunities, as they can lead to unexpected and rewarding career paths. Seeking advice from career coaches or mentors can provide guidance tailored to one's unique situation, helping to navigate the complexities of the job market with confidence. Ultimately, re-entering the job market is a process that benefits from preparation, positivity, and patience, as each step taken is a move towards achieving one's professional goals.

Embrace this new chapter in your life with enthusiasm, and let the knowledge you've gained illuminate your path to achievement. You learned that you are more resilient than you ever thought possible. Your new career path is not just a job change; it's a chance to redefine your professional identity and leave a lasting impact on your life.

The Bible is often regarded as a guiding light in the lives of many, offering wisdom and direction through its teachings. It is seen as a spiritual compass that helps believers navigate the complexities of life, providing principles and parables that resonate with various aspects of human experience. The Scriptures are considered by some to be divinely inspired, containing insights that are timeless and relevant across generations. For those who follow its teachings, the Bible can serve as a roadmap, illuminating the path toward personal growth, ethical behavior, and a deeper understanding of one's purpose and place in the world. It is a source of comfort and strength for many, offering hope and guidance in times of uncertainty and challenge.

Congratulations on this new and exciting chapter in your life. As it says in the Bible, Isaiah 43:18–19 (NIV), "Forget the former things; do not dwell on the past. See, I am doing a new thing! Now it springs up; do you not perceive it? I am making a way in the wilderness and streams in the wasteland."

HR insider tip. *Continuing the job search even after receiving an offer letter is a prudent strategy. It's not uncommon for candidates to experience setbacks after seemingly successful interviews where promises of positions and start dates vanish without further communication. This can leave job seekers in a difficult position if they have halted their job search strategy. It's advisable to maintain an active pursuit of employment opportunities until the new role has officially begun. This approach ensures that one's career prospects remain open, providing a safety net should any unexpected changes occur with the initial job offer.*

Chapter 12:
Continue to Learn

"You will rejoice in all you have accomplished because the LORD your God has blessed you."

Deuteronomy 12:7 (NLT)

In the modern workforce, lifelong learning is a fundamental component of career development. It encompasses the continuous acquisition of knowledge and skills throughout an individual's life, particularly in response to rapidly evolving job markets and technological advancements. This concept has gained significant traction as a means to maintain competitiveness and relevance in one's career.

Lifelong learners are often seen as more adaptable, capable of navigating changes, and better positioned for career advancement. The pursuit of lifelong learning is not just about formal education; it extends to informal and nonformal learning opportunities, such as professional workshops, online courses, and self-directed study. It is a proactive approach to career development, where individuals take charge of their learning journey, seeking out new knowledge and experiences that align with their career goals and personal interests.

By embracing a growth mindset, lifelong learners remain open to new ideas and challenges, viewing failures as opportunities for growth rather than setbacks. This mindset fosters resilience and a willingness to step outside one's comfort zone, which are crucial traits in today's dynamic work environment. Organizations also play a role in promoting lifelong learning by creating cultures that encourage and support employee development. This can be achieved through mentorship programs, providing access to learning resources, and recognizing the achievements of employees who demonstrate a commitment to continuous learning. Ultimately, lifelong learning is about staying curious, engaged, and motivated throughout one's career, ensuring that both individuals and organizations can thrive in an ever-changing world.

Lifelong learning is not only beneficial for individual career progression but also for organizations seeking to innovate and stay ahead of industry trends. It contributes to a more skilled and versatile workforce that is capable of tackling complex problems and driving business success. Therefore, both employees and employers must recognize the value of lifelong learning and actively foster an environment where continuous personal and professional development is not just encouraged but expected.

The dynamic and enriching journey of lifelong learning extends beyond the traditional classroom setting. It is a self-motivated pursuit of knowledge that spans one's entire life. It offers a pathway to personal fulfillment and professional development. This form of education is not confined to formal institutions but flourishes in a variety of settings, embracing all ages and stages of life. It empowers individuals to adapt to the ever-evolving demands of the workforce, equipping them with the skills necessary to thrive in a rapidly changing world.

Lifelong learning fosters a culture of curiosity and continuous improvement, encouraging people to explore new interests, develop new skills, and expand their horizons. It is a testament to the human spirit's unyielding desire to grow and learn, reflecting a commitment to self-improvement, including spiritual and societal advancement. The quest for knowledge and personal growth is a fundamental aspect of the human experience. Throughout history, this drive has propelled humanity to explore the unknown, innovate, and push the boundaries of what is possible. It's the force behind our greatest scientific discoveries, artistic masterpieces, and philosophical inquiries. This innate desire not only enriches individual lives but also advances societies by fostering a culture of continuous learning and improvement. As we look to the future, it is this very spirit that will continue to shape our world and increase our self-growth and awareness while leading us to new horizons.

The Holy Spirit's indwelling within us is a profound aspect of Christian theology as the Holy Spirit resides within believers, guiding and transforming them from within. This belief is rooted in various scriptural references that describe the body as a temple for the Holy Spirit and emphasize the transformative power of the Spirit's presence. The indwelling is seen as a guarantee of God's ownership and a continuous source of spiritual renewal and strength, providing comfort in trials and sustaining believers in afflictions. It's a cornerstone of faith that underscores the intimate relationship between the divine and the human, reflecting a deep, personal connection that is both empowering and sanctifying.

The pursuit of learning is a profound journey that not only enriches the mind and soul but also enhances the quality of life. Engaging in continuous learning has been shown to bring about a multitude of benefits, contributing to a more enjoyable and fulfilling existence. It fosters a sense of accomplishment and confidence as one deepens self-awareness and acquires new knowledge and skills. This process of learning can be deeply satisfying, offering a sense of progress and accomplishments in both personal and spiritual growth. Moreover, learning cultivates a curious and active mind, which is essential for adapting to new challenges and solving problems creatively. It also encourages social interaction and community involvement, as shared educational experiences can lead to meaningful connections with others. Furthermore, learning can be fun as it often involves exploring one's passions and interests. The act of learning itself can be intrinsically rewarding, providing a sense of purpose and direction in life.

Our perspectives change when we follow God's will and live according to His divine plan. Our vision expands, and we begin to look at life not in terms of what we can do but what God can do through us. Once we start following God's direction, we realize that nothing can destroy, discourage, disappoint, or defeat us.

Additionally, following God's direction contributes to mental well-being, as it can help maintain cognitive function and mental agility throughout one's lifespan. The intersection of spirituality and mental well-being is a profound and complex topic. Many find that their spiritual beliefs and practices can play a significant role in their mental health. For instance, "God's will" is often interpreted as a guiding force that can provide comfort and direction during challenging times. This belief can foster a sense of purpose and hope, which are essential components of psychological resilience. The spiritual practice of prayer can contribute to a sense of peace and well-being, offering a way to cope with stress and anxiety. It's important to recognize that spirituality can be a source of strength for many. Combining spiritual practices with mental health interventions can offer a holistic approach to well-being, aligning one's faith with the care for their mental state. This holistic approach is reflected in various resources and discussions that explore the relationship between faith, understanding God's will, and maintaining mental health. Spiritual learning is also a lifelong process that can significantly contribute to a richer, more vibrant life experience.

The path of spiritual development is a deeply personal and transformative journey that encompasses a broad spectrum of experiences and stages. It often begins with an awakening, a realization that there is more to life than the material world and its pursuits. This discovery may lead to a quest for deeper understanding and connection with the self, others, and God.

Similarly, the spiritual journey is seen as a progression from fear and separation to love, connectedness, and expansion, with each stage offering unique challenges and opportunities for growth. Spiritual development is not linear but rather a complex, evolving process that can involve introspection, meditation, study, and the practice of various spiritual disciplines. It is a journey toward self-realization, peace, and empathy, where one seeks to align with their innermost values and purpose. Ultimately, it is a path that leads to the expansion of consciousness and the embrace of a more holistic, integrated view of existence.

The continuous pursuit of lifelong learning in our spiritual lives, careers, and self-development takes on many forms. From formal education to informal experiences such as travel, hobbies, and cultural exchanges, it's about expanding horizons, not just professionally but personally and also spiritually. It's accessible to all, regardless of age or background. The benefits of lifelong learning include increased self-confidence, resilience, and adaptability. Lifelong learning is not just about career advancement; it's about enriching one's life and broadening one's perspective on the world. It's a journey that can lead to unexpected career discoveries and opportunities, making life more fulfilling and enjoyable.

The pursuit of personal expansion is a journey that encompasses the mind, the acquisition of knowledge, and the essence of one's life. Expanding your thinking involves embracing a mindset that is open to new ideas, perspectives, and ways of understanding the world around us. It's about allowing curiosity to lead the way and being willing to step outside of comfort zones to challenge preconceived notions. It's not just about accumulating facts; it's about engaging with information critically and creatively, seeking out diverse sources, and applying knowledge in innovative ways. This approach to learning fosters a growth mindset, where challenges are seen as opportunities to evolve.

Expanding your life means taking the insights gained from broadened thinking and learning to enrich every aspect of your existence. It's about making conscious choices that align with your values, goals, desires, and aspirations. It also includes building meaningful relationships and contributing positively to the communities you are part of. This holistic expansion can lead to a more fulfilling and purposeful life marked by continuous personal development and a deep sense of achievement.

The transition to living a fuller life is not just about a new job or promotion; it's about continuing to discover your purpose and passions and how they align with the work you will be doing. May this new beginning bring you fulfillment and opportunities to use your God-given talents and abilities in new and meaningful ways.

Continue to Learn

God commands us to be responsible with our abilities, resources, and gifts. Here are examples of Scripture that encourage believers to use their skills for the glory of God and to benefit others.

- The parable of the talents in the Bible (Matthew 25:14–30) teaches about using and developing one's talents.
- Proverbs 22:29 emphasizes the importance of honing one's skills and excelling in them.
- Ephesians 2:10 mentions that believers are created for good works, which can involve utilizing their talents and skills.
- First Peter 4:10 instructs believers to use their gifts to serve others as good stewards of God's grace.

Take some time and reflect on how you can apply the teachings of these scriptures to your own life to develop and utilize your talents and skills effectively.

As the journey continues, these learned skills and self-discoveries will be the foundation for future successes, whether in this job or in your life. It's a continuous process of learning, growing, and achieving, with each new role offering unique challenges and opportunities to evolve professionally, personally, and spiritually.

The VIP Job Search

The duration of searching for that dream job, searching for career advancement, or being unemployed can indeed be influenced by an individual's adaptability and willingness to learn. The job market is dynamic and affected by various factors such as economic conditions, technological advancements, and global competition. Research indicates that during economic downturns, unemployment durations can increase significantly. Additionally, the rise of automation and the need for new skill sets can make it challenging for those who are not open to learning and change. Lifelong learning is essential in this context, as it allows individuals to stay relevant and competitive in the job market. Embracing a mindset of continuous personal and professional development can be a decisive factor in shortening the period of unemployment, career advancement, and obtaining new opportunities.

A mindset of continuous learning is a strategic approach to personal and professional development. By consistently acquiring new skills, such as mastering a software program or enhancing your proficiency in Microsoft Office, you not only stay relevant in an ever-evolving job market but also open doors to new opportunities and challenges. Setting a goal to add one or two new skills to your repertoire annually is a tangible and achievable objective that can lead to significant growth over time. This practice enriches your skill set by showing employers you are adaptable and innovative. These are two qualities highly valued in the modern workplace.

Continue to Learn

The journey of job searching is a transformative experience, extending beyond professional development into personal and spiritual growth. The skills, resilience, and self-confidence built during this time often lead to a positive ripple effect in various aspects of life. It's a period of learning, self-discovery, and, at times, spiritual deepening. The encouragement to remain hopeful and patient is a powerful reminder that opportunities can arise when least expected. The sentiment that God's plan unfolds in His time can provide comfort and strength to continue forward, reinforcing the idea that perseverance and faith go hand in hand in the pursuit of future endeavors.

The job market is dynamic and an ever-evolving landscape, reflecting the constant changes in technology, economy, and societal needs. The lessons learned during the job search process are invaluable, offering insights into personal strengths, areas for improvement, and the adaptability required to thrive in such an environment. It's essential to carry these lessons forward, not just as a memory but as a toolkit for professional development. As the job market continues to diverge from past experiences, these personal insights become the guiding principles for navigating one's career path, ensuring readiness for future opportunities and challenges. Remembering and applying what you've learned about yourself and the job search process is crucial for long-term success and fulfillment in your career.

The transition from job seeker to new employee is a critical phase in one's professional journey. It's essential to carry forward the lessons learned during the job search into the new role. As a new employee, it's important to understand the company culture, establish relationships, and exceed the expectations set for your position. The mindset of a lifelong learner will find that the investment in your education pays dividends in the form of career resilience and satisfaction.

As traditional corporate support structures like tuition reimbursement fade, the emphasis on skill development becomes more pronounced. Companies are investing in training and development programs that offer immediate applicability and measurable benefits. This trend underscores the importance of the willingness to continuously acquire new skills.

Individuals are increasingly taking charge of their professional development, recognizing that lifelong learning is essential for staying relevant in a rapidly evolving job market. This proactive approach is not just about maintaining employment; it's about seizing control of one's career trajectory and personal growth. Learning, of course, is not just a means to an end. It's a continuous journey of one's life and career. The message is clear: to thrive in today's world, one must be an agile learner, ready to pursue knowledge and opportunities with determination and resilience.

Continue to Learn

In today's rapidly evolving workplace, the ability to transform obstacles into opportunities is invaluable. A culture of continuous learning is becoming integral to job engagement and organizational success. Companies are increasingly recognizing the importance of investing in relevant training programs to empower their employees. This not only fosters personal growth and job satisfaction but also aligns with the company's strategic goals. Skill development is not just a pathway to individual excellence but a cornerstone of organizational resilience. As employers strive to reduce turnover costs, they are beginning to understand that creating a learning culture is not an expense but a strategic investment. This investment not only equips employees to make meaningful contributions more quickly but also enhances their loyalty and commitment to the organization, ultimately leading to a more dynamic, skilled, and engaged workforce. Taking ownership of one's learning journey empowers employees to identify and pursue relevant courses that align with their career goals rather than waiting for employer directives. Key drivers of success are adaptability and continuous learning.

The continuous evolution of industries and the rapid pace of technological advancements necessitate a culture of perpetual learning within organizations. To thrive in the future, companies must foster an environment where learning is not only encouraged but integrated into the daily workflow. This involves creating accessible and relevant training programs that align with both the company's strategic goals and the individual's career aspirations.

For professionals, rekindling a passion for learning is crucial for career advancement. The knowledge and skills that were pertinent during college years may no longer suffice in today's dynamic job market. It's essential to stay abreast of the latest trends and terminologies in one's field, as these are often indicators of where the industry is heading.

An increase in corporate training budgets reflects the growing recognition and value of workforce development. Investing in employee education is not just about filling knowledge gaps; it's about shaping a workforce that is agile, innovative, and capable of driving the company forward in an uncertain future. Continuous learning is the cornerstone of both personal growth and organizational success.

In today's fast-paced professional environment, a self-directed approach to career development is indeed crucial. Crafting a personal improvement plan is a strategic move that can lead to significant advancements in one's career. Focusing on enhancing skills such as PowerPoint, Excel, and overall MS Office proficiency not only boosts performance but also showcases a commitment to continuous learning. Mastery of these tools, coupled with in-depth knowledge of employer-specific software, positions an individual as an invaluable asset to any team.

Continue to Learn

The pursuit of knowledge across various domains is a commendable approach to personal and professional development. It's essential to view learning not as a chore but as an investment in oneself that can lead to greater opportunities and career growth. Embracing the unknown and fostering innovation through new experiences can lead to profound personal transformation and the discovery of untapped potential.

Landing a job in today's competitive market requires a commitment to lifelong learning and the continuous enhancement of both hard and soft skills. Hard skills, such as technical abilities and specialized knowledge, are often acquired through formal education and training and can be crucial for meeting the specific demands of a job. On the other hand, soft skills, which encompass personal attributes like communication, leadership, and emotional intelligence, are equally important for career success and can often be developed through self-reflection, practice, and feedback. To stay relevant and adaptable in a rapidly evolving workplace, professionals should seek out opportunities for learning and growth, such as online courses, workshops, and mentorship programs. This not only helps in keeping one's skill set current but also demonstrates a proactive attitude toward personal and professional development, a quality highly valued by employers.

If it has been some time since you have taken any type of

course, you may be perceived as "stuck" or "rigid" in your way of thinking. In today's world of work, the economy is seeking "flexibility," which is a very valuable soft skill for employers.

Gain an edge over your career by learning new skills while improving on others. Use your time productively and wisely. Take classes online through LinkedIn, your local community college, or through your local library. If unemployed, check with your local unemployment office for a listing of in-person or online classes available.

It is imperative in today's job market that individuals continue with lifelong learning goals. For example, if your technology job skills are not up-to-date, you are unable to compete with other job seekers. Do not assume at any point that you have arrived or are an expert in your field. Keep an open mind and improve your PowerPoint skills, your Excel skills, and your public speaking skills. It's about adding value to the employer and keeping yourself marketable. Be proactive. Keep improving your skills and remain open to opportunities.

Make sure your continued education goals and lifelong learning goals are in writing. Make a plan and write it down. Design a personalized career "success plan" and focus on that plan. What does your future life look like? Commit to your plan and explore options. Remember, the journey to a satisfying life is ongoing, and it's important to stay adaptable and willing to learn and grow

Continue to Learn

as your interests evolve. Life is dynamic, and in the process of living life, we change as people. The job that we worked so hard to get may not be the job we are looking for in a few years.

A success plan is a strategic framework that individuals or organizations use to set and achieve goals. It typically involves identifying objectives, outlining the steps needed to reach them, and establishing metrics to measure progress. For students, a success plan might include academic goals, extracurricular activities, and personal development milestones, serving as a dynamic record of their strengths, interests, and needs both in and out of school. In a business context, a success plan can detail a company's tasks and actions to achieve specific aims, such as increasing brand awareness or customer engagement. These plans are not static; they are living documents that should be updated as new information becomes available or when goals evolve. Success plans are also used in customer service to align services and solutions with the unique goals and needs of each client, setting clear expectations and adapting strategies to ensure progress toward desired outcomes. Essentially, a success plan is a roadmap for success, tailored to the individual or organization's specific context and objectives.

Pray without ceasing. Acknowledge God daily for the gifts He has given you in your life. God gave your life, which is a huge blessing within itself. People will disappoint you; people will let you down. God will never disappoint. He is the same yesterday, today and tomorrow.

May God bless you in all your life's endeavors. I pray that this new beginning brings you awareness, fulfillment, and opportunities for you to use your God-given talents and abilities in meaningful ways. Remember, you and God are a majority.

HR insider tip. In today's dynamic job market, staying marketable is crucial, and lifelong learning is the key to maintaining and enhancing one's employability. This encompasses not only professional development through updating skills and embracing new technologies and trends but also personal growth. Employers are increasingly valuing soft skills and seeking candidates who not only fit the technical requirements of a job but also the company culture. This holistic approach to career development ensures that individuals are not just suitable for the job today but are adaptable and valuable assets for the future